Creative Stitching on Paper

Creative Stitching on Paper

40 Beautiful Projects, From Scrapbook Pages to Chinese Lanterns

Joanne O'Sullivan

LARK BOOKS

A Division of Sterling Publishing Co., Inc.
New York

Art Director: Susan McBride & Kathleen Holmes

Cover Designer: Barbara Zaretsky

Photography: www.keithwright.com

Illustrations: Orrin Lundgren

Associate Editor: Susan Kieffer

Associate Art Director: Shannon Yokeley

Art Production Assistant: Jeff Hamilton

Editorial Assistance: Delores Gosnell

Library of Congress Cataloging-in-Publication Data

O'Sullivan, Joanne.
    Creative stitching on paper : from scrapbook pages to Chinese lanterns, 40 beautiful projects
/ by Joanne O'Sullivan.—1st ed.
        p.   cm.
    Includes index.
    ISBN 1-57990-699-0
    1. Needlework—Patterns.   I. Title.
TT760.O89 2006
746.4—dc22

                            2005017766

10 9 8 7 6 5 4 3 2 1

First Edition

Published by Lark Books, A Division of Sterling Publishing Co., Inc. 387 Park Avenue South,
New York, N.Y. 10016

Distributed in Canada by Sterling Publishing, c/o Canadian Manda Group, 165 Dufferin Street,
Toronto, Ontario, Canada M6K 3H6

Distributed in the U.K. by Guild of Master Craftsman Publications Ltd., Castle Place, 166 High
Street, Lewes, East Sussex, England BN7 1XU Tel: (+ 44) 1273 477374, Fax: (+ 44) 1273 478606,
e-mail: pubs@thegmcgroup.com, Web: www.gmcpublications.com

Distributed in Australia by Capricorn Link (Australia) Pty Ltd., P.O. Box 704, Windsor,
NSW 2756 Australia

If you have questions or comments about this book, please contact:
Lark Books
67 Broadway
Asheville, NC 28801
(828) 253-0467

Manufactured in China

ISBN 13: 978-1-57990-699-3
ISBN 10: 1-57990-699-0

For information about custom editions, special sales, premiums, and corporate purchases, please
contact Sterling Special Sales Department at (800) 805-5489 or specialsales@sterlingpub.com.

Contents

Introduction

Paper and sewing: one is so ephemeral, one so permanent. The combination of this material and this technique may seem unexpected, but paper crafters, scrapbookers, and sewers alike are discovering that it's also refreshingly original, opening up lots of new possibilities for creativity.

While sewing on paper may seem like a new idea, it's been done for centuries: ancient books were bound by sewing through parchment or vellum, and remarkably, some of them have endured through time. Paper isn't necessarily flimsy and disposable—if it's made from material with long fibers, it can be just as strong as fabric, or even stronger. In fact, many projects that can be made by sewing on fabric can just as easily be made of paper. Whether you're looking for a decorative effect, a functional binding, or both, stitches help you achieve paper crafting effects impossible to get with glue or folding. And with so many beautiful papers out there in irresistible patterns, textures, and colors, why not give it a try?

Before diving into the projects, get acquainted with the properties of different types of papers and threads in the Getting Started section. You may be surprised at how many different kinds of paper can stand up to being poked and sewn without tearing. In this section, you'll also learn about which needles and other tools are best to use for stitching on paper. Even the most basic sewing machines offer a few decorative stitches, and higher-end models offer dozens. Hand sewing is a great option for delicate papers, creating a handmade look, or for adding buttons or beads. An illustrated stitch gallery shows you how to create some of the most common embroidery stitches by hand. You'll refer back to this section when you need to use one of these stitches to create the projects.

Whether you're a hand or machine sewer, you'll find tips here that will lead to successful results.

Once you've experimented with the materials and techniques, try your hand at the more than 40 projects that run the gamut from cards and gifts, home accents, and scrapbook-page ideas, to holiday and party decorations. Create an heirloom-quality family tree with gorgeous printed papers and a delicate feather stitch. Delight new parents with a baby mobile made from pastel-print scrapbook papers and an ordinary hanger. Cover a less-than-perfect view with a curtain made from exquisite leaf-print paper shapes sewn together with jute cord. There are lots of templates at the back of the book to accompany the instructions. After you've tried a few projects, you'll find yourself looking at paper in a whole new light.

I hope you'll use this book to come up with designs of your own—simple creations for a special occasion or sophisticated ones meant to last for years. Artisically stitching on paper is easier than you might think and more fun than you can imagine.

Getting Started

Materials

There are a lot of variables involved in choosing your materials for a stitched-paper project: the weight of the paper; the thickness of the thread or yarn; the size of the needle, its tip, and its eye; the length of the stitch; and the tension in your sewing machine. Just like sewing on fabric, you'll need to become familiar with the specific characteristics of the materials you use. Experiment with different combinations of paper, thread, and needles to find out what effects you'll get. The following section gives you a starting point for considering which materials and tools to use.

Papers

From exquisite handmade unryu paper (also known as rice or mulberry paper) to reliable old card stock, you can use a variety of papers for your stitching project. The best way to find a paper you like is by experimenting. In general, the more like fabric a paper is, the easier it will be to sew on. You can work with paper of almost any weight. Tissuey-texture paper may tear, but don't rule out delicate, lacey, woven papers, such as washi. If the fibers in a paper are long enough, it can easily be used for hand-sewn projects, or even stitched in a machine.

Look for acid and lignin-free papers if you're creating a project that you want to last for many years, and consider the colorfastness of a paper if your project will be continually exposed to daylight over time.

Handmade papers. Any "dense" handmade paper—that is, one with a high fiber content—is appropriate for a stitching project. The most delicate of papers, such as Japanese washi paper, may seem intimidatingly fragile, but it can easily be used for stitching projects because of the length and strength of the fibers. Other woven papers, such as unryu, more durable Indian coconut paper, and Nepalese lokta, have a woven, bark-like texture that makes them quite strong, so they work well for stitched projects, too. Any handmade paper featuring silk, cotton, linen, hemp or other plant fibers will work well for stitching projects with slender needles and thin thread. Handmade mica, banana, and mango paper, although heavier, are not as strongly woven as some of the more delicate handmade papers, so they should probably not be used for machine sewing. Papers with embedded leaves or plant material can be used for hand-sewn projects as long as the add-ins are not too thick—seeds and leaves can break small needles. Pierce the paper in advance and use large needles for best results.

Rag paper. Similar to watercolor paper, this cotton- or linen-fiber paper comes in various weights with different levels of "tooth" (surface texture). This paper is sturdy enough for stitching, but you should use small needles to avoid creating big holes, which may spread over time.

Suede, velvet, velour, and "leatherette" papers. These papers are named after the fabrics that their texture resembles. They are best suited to hand sewing and simple stitches, such as the running stitch. They're popular for use in journal and bookbinding projects.

Vellum. Vellum has a crisp texture and therefore isn't as forgiving as some other papers when it comes to stitching. If you're machine sewing over vellum, you should go quite slowly. Hand-sewing with vellum is fine, as long as you use a smallish, sharp needle. Vellum is a popular choice for adding windows or pockets to cards, journals, and scrapbook pages and for creating an overlay for patterned papers.

Decorative papers. "Decorative paper" is a term used to describe any printed or patterned paper (usually machine-made) that can be used for arts and crafts projects. These papers are usually medium-weight; they are heavier than wrapping paper but lighter than a handmade woven paper such as lokta. These papers are versatile and can be used for hand or machine sewing. Look for patterns that won't overwhelm your stitching.

Scrapbooking papers. Although they're stationery-weight papers, scrapbooking papers are great for both machine- and hand-stitching projects.

Card stock. Also referred to as cover-weight paper, card stock is the workhorse of papers. It's machine-made and available in a variety of weights, from flexible to almost cardboard consistency. It's inexpensive and easily found at craft and office supply stores. Card stock is perfect for creating durable stitched-paper projects.

Threads and Yarn

Depending on your choice of paper, you can use any type of thread, from ordinary sewing thread to embroidery floss, as well as raffia and ribbon for hand-sewn projects. Machine sewing limits you a bit in terms of thread type and weight, but it offers you a lot of different color choices.

Sewing thread. Rayon, cotton, and polyester threads work equally well with paper.

Pearl cotton thread. This thread is thicker than sewing thread and consists of twisted strands that can't be divided. It's quite strong, so it's a good choice for projects that will be handled a lot or need extra-strong binding. This thread should only be used for hand-sewing projects.

Embroidery floss. A popular choice for hand-sewn projects, floss comes in a wide variety of colors and can be used to create different effects. Each skein of floss is made up of six strands. For a delicate design, use two or three strands, or use all six for more heft. It's fun to use strands from different colors of floss for an interesting woven effect.

Metallic thread. Because it's heavier and more brittle than sewing thread, metallic thread should be matched with a strong paper. Don't use it for machine sewing unless the machine manufacturer specifies that it's compatible.

Buttonhole or carpet thread. This waxed cotton thread is good for hand-sewing projects where strength is key, such as stitching pamphlets for bookbinding. Use it for hand-stitching projects only.

Yarn. Most lighter-weight natural-fiber yarns can be used for hand-stitched projects, although you might find yourself lacing rather than sewing them. Some will fit through tapestry needles.

Jute and raffia. Either of these natural fibers will work for hand stitching on medium- to heavyweight paper. For best results, pre-pierce the holes you'll sew through with this thick material.

Ribbon. A thin ribbon can be used with a tapestry needle for sewing through pre-pierced holes. Thicker ribbons are good for lacing through punched holes. Notch the end of the ribbon so that it's easier to thread through the eye of the needle.

Wire. Very thin beading wire can be used to attach beads, buttons, and other trinkets to a paper project. Obviously, you'll need to look for wire that's sturdy enough to hold your add-on, but won't weigh down your paper.

Specialty Materials
Fusible Interfacing

Just like fabric, you can attach fusible interfacing to paper to make it sturdier. This is a good solution if you have a fairly lightweight piece of paper that you want to use for a project that will receive a lot of handling. To attach the interfacing, follow the manufacturer's instructions, but keep in mind that you'll need to use a lower temperature setting on your iron than you would for fabric. Test a piece of the paper you want to use first.

Tools

Needles

Your choice of needle will largely depend on your choice of paper and thread. If your paper is delicate, you'll need a slender, sharp needle. For heavier-weight paper, you can use a large-eyed needle with a blunter tip. A general sewing needle will do for most hand-stitching projects.

Keep in mind that sewing into paper dulls your needles much more quickly than sewing into fabric, so you'll want to have a stash of different needles on hand if you plan to do a lot of stitching on paper.

Embroidery needles.

Although they come in varying lengths, these needles with sharp points and long eyes work well with embroidery floss and are recommended with papers on the thin side.

Sharps.

A pointy, thin, needle with a round eye used for hand sewing, This type of needle is great for sewing into thin papers with thin thread.

Tapestry needles.

Tapestry needles have blunt points and large eyes; they are good for yarn, pearl cotton, jute, raffia, ribbon, and multiple strands of embroidery floss. They're also great for pre-piercing your paper.

Darners.

These are strong needles with large eyes and are good for use with thicker papers and threads. They can also be used for piercing holes in paper before sewing.

Sewing Machine

Any machine can be used to sew on paper. The trick is to experiment with your machine to see how different papers respond to it. You can use a mini sewing machine for convenience, but you'll be limited in terms of decorative stitches because most have only straight stitch.

Specialty Tools

Dressmaker's pin.

This is useful for poking holes in paper to map out your design before sewing it.

Awl.

An awl can be used for poking holes in paper, especially when you'll be poking through several layers. This tool is often used for bookbinding or making journals, because those projects often require folded pamphlets of paper.

Hole punch.

It's a good idea to have hole punches of various sizes (from micro-punch on up) on hand when stitching on paper. You'll definitely need them if you're using a heavier fiber, such as raffia or jute, or a heavier yarn.

Paper-piercing tool.

While needles, dressmaking pins, awls, hole punches, and other tools may be used for making holes to sew through, there are tools made specifically for paper piercing available at craft stores. This special tool is useful for making holes of uniform size through papers of various weights.

Dressmaker's wheel.

This can be a useful tool for creating closely spaced holes for abstract designs and meandering lines. Keep in mind though, that closely spaced holes can damage fragile paper, so limit your use of this tool to sturdy paper.

Cutting mat, mouse pad, or magazine.

A soft object such as one of these items will support the paper while you poke holes in it for sewing.

Techniques

The first rule of stitching on paper is always to test your stitching on a scrap of the same type you'll use for your project. The second rule is to experiment and have fun. After that, there are no rules!

In general, the sewing you do will fall into two categories: stitches that hold an item together and stitches that are purely decorative. Of course, some stitches can be both. The nature of your project, your personal preference, and your materials will determine whether you need to hand sew or machine sew. Hand stitching and machine stitching have distinctive looks, so one type might lend itself more naturally to your project than the other. Again, many projects are a combination of both. Certain stitches are also a natural for certain projects. Featherstitch and fern stitch, for example, are great for nature-inspired designs, while blanket stitch gives a rustic, country look to a project. The projects in this book are great for kick-starting your imagination. The techniques described in the following section can be applied to a variety of projects and will help you get started stitching on paper.

Preparing Your Design

Even if you're using a fairly heavy-weight paper, it's best to avoid stitch-heavy designs that will weigh down the paper. While you're still learning about your materials, try simple borders or outlines first before moving onto more complicated motifs.

Once you have an idea in mind, you can start the process of getting it onto your paper.

If you're going for an informal and artistic look, you can always create your design spontaneously. You can also pencil a design freehand onto your paper, then sew along the outline.

If you're hand-sewing, you can pre-pierce the design into the paper (see page 13).

Another way to transfer your design is to create it first on tracing paper, then lay the tracing paper on top of the paper you'll use, securing it at the edges with low-tack tape. Then you can punch through the design at intervals (not too close together), thus transferring the design to the paper. You will, of course, need to remove the tracing paper before you begin to stitch.

Hand Sewing

Hand sewing is great for projects involving delicate paper, metallic or heavy-fiber threads, or specific embroidery stitches that you can't get from a machine.

When hand sewing on paper, it's best to use a longer stitch length and keep you're the lines of your stitches spaced well apart from each other. Too many tight stitches will weigh down the paper and lead to tearing.

Don't "knot" the thread as you would when sewing on fabric. The best way to secure loose ends is with some kind of adhesive, such as strong glue, glue dots, or a small piece of archival tape.

Pre-piercing Paper

If you're looking for a consistent outcome, or if you're stitching with floss or a thicker fiber, or into a fairly heavy paper, it's a good idea to pre-pierce your design into the paper before you start to sew it. But remember, once you poke a hole in paper, it's there for good. That's why you should always do a test scrap in advance.

Choose a piercing tool most appropriate for the thickness of your thread. If you try to pull a thick thread through a small hole, the paper will tear and the thread will fray. A straight pin or needle may create a big enough hole for sewing thread, but you'll need a blunt-tip needle or a piercing tool for floss or pearl-cotton thread. For larger holes, use an appropriately sized hole punch. Again, you'll

want to consider the look you're trying to achieve before choosing a tool.

Careful marking will also lead to more successful results.

If you're hand-sewing, follow these steps:

Use a pencil to mark where you'll place your stitches. Poke holes from 1/8 inch (3 mm) to 1 inch (2.5 cm) apart, depending on the design and the size of stitch you want. Bring your needle up from behind the paper into the first hole and follow along your design.

Attaching Beads, Buttons, and Charms

While adding heavy beads closely spaced together is probably not a good idea for paper projects, a few beads and buttons here and there add a nice layer of dimension to a stitched-paper project.

You can attach single sequins, charms, beads, and buttons the same way you would to fabric—by starting at the back, threading through the hole or holes, going through to the back again, and then knotting in the back. Then just add a dab of glue to keep the knot from coming undone. It's a good idea to pre-punch the holes you'll sew through.

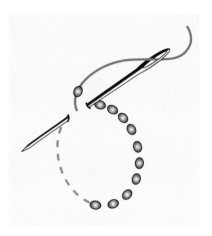

If you're going to add more than one bead, button, or sequin, use a beading needle and this method: Sew each bead on separately, threading it onto the needle, poking it through, and securing it with a backstitch before moving on to the next add-in. A thin needle, strong thread, and beads with a small opening are recommended for paper projects. Instead of thread, you may choose to use monofilament or wire. Try adding a dab of strong glue in the back to secure the final knot in place.

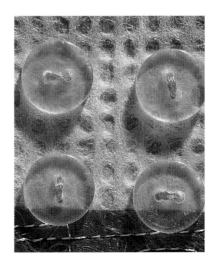

Machine Sewing on Paper

Machine sewing on paper is much the same as sewing on fabric; if you've chosen an appropriate paper, it can be done on any sewing machine. High-end sewing machines offer a wide variety of decorative stitches, but even the simplest machines offer a few alternatives (such as zigzag or featherstitches), so you can achieve a wider range of effects than you can with hand-stitching. Machine-stitching is a lot faster than hand-stitching, too, so it's ideal for larger projects. Although much will be determined by the machine you use, here are a few points to consider when machine sewing on paper.

Use a small needle and a slow machine speed. Even if you're sewing on sturdy paper, a fast machine speed may permanently damage the fibers of the paper.

It's important to keep a loose stitch density. A very dense stitch, such as satin stitch, will weigh down the paper and possibly tear it, so it's not a good choice. If you're using

embroidery software, delete the underlay stitch to reduce the stitch density.

Use the longest stitch possible, because short stitches placed close together can cause the paper to tear.

Before you start to stitch, make sure your bobbin has enough thread to finish the job. If your bobbin runs out of thread midway, you'll be left with holes in the paper that you'll have to work to conceal.

Don't try to machine stitch more than three layers of paper together at one time.

It's a good idea to test out how your machine works on a particular paper so you can adjust your stitch length and tension as needed.

Remember: Test every stitch on a scrap of the paper you'll use before you begin your final project.

Also remember that stitching on paper dulls needles, so you'll need to keep a supply of extra needles on hand.

Adding a Backing to Stitched Paper

To give a flimsy piece of stitched paper more heft, and to hide your stitches, you can attach, either with stitching or with glue, another piece of paper to the back. If you're doing it to hide stitches, use any decorative paper, but if you're doing it to make a piece of stitched paper less flimsy, use something such as card stock on the back.

Of course, you can also do your stitching on one piece of paper, then adhere the stitched paper to another piece of paper. This is a good strategy.

Stitch Gallery

Running Stitch

This is the simplest stitch, used for creating straight lines of any length. Simply take your needle through the wrong side to the right side of your work and stitch, making a stitch to the desired length, then bring the needle back through.

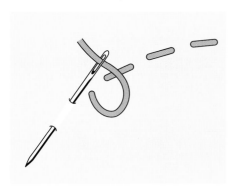

Backstitch

The backstitch is useful when you need a strong, durable stitch. Bring the needle up to the right of your starting point, then place it back into the starting point. Bring it back up just to the right of the first point where you brought it up, then go back in at the first point you brought it up. Continue making stitches of uniform size.

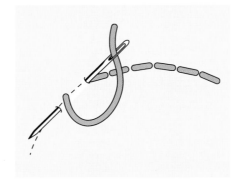

Blanket Stitch

Working from left to right, bring the needle to the right side of the paper on the edge. Make an upright stitch to the right with the needle pointed down. Catch the thread under the point of the needle as you come out on the edge.

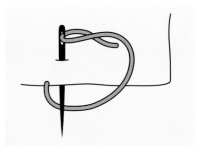

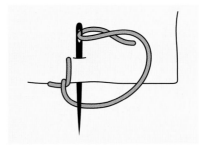

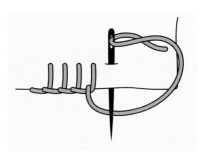

French Knot

Starting on the right side of your work, wrap the thread twice around the point of your needle, pull it tight, and insert the needle next to where it came out. Hold the thread taut to form a knot, and pull the needle through to the wrong side of the fabric to secure it.

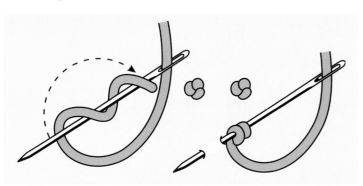

Cross-Stitch

This stitch looks just as it sounds—it creates a basic X. Try to keep the length of your stitches regular and the slant of the stitches even. Bring your needle from the lower right-hand corner up on a diagonal and reinsert it. Come back up again on the bottom line, to the left of your first stitch, and continue the process until you have the number of diagonal lines you want. Then start in the lower left-hand corner and cross over the diagonals you previously made, essentially reversing the process.

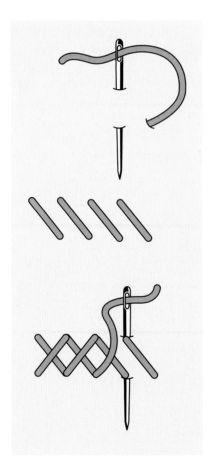

Featherstitch

Bring the needle up at your first hole. Hold down the thread with your thumb, bring the needle in, and then bring it up, making a modest loop. (Keep the loop under the needle.)

Repeat the stitch below and to the left. Bring the needle up again. Holding down the thread with your thumb, bring the needle in, making another modest loop. (Keep the loop under the needle.)

Repeat the stitch below and to the right. Bring the needle up. Hold down the thread with your thumb, and bring the needle in, making a modest loop. (Keep the loop under the needle.)

Repeat, alternating stitches. To finish, make a vertical stitch over a loop.

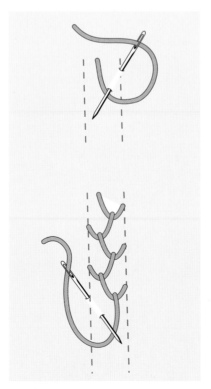

Fern Stitch

A variation of the featherstitch, this is a great stitch for imitating the look of leaves or vines. The stitches radiate out from a central curved line. Bring the needle to the surface a little bit from the end of your vine, and make a straight stitch. Make a diagonal stitch to the right of the line, starting at the far end of the diagonal, and bring it back in at the centerline. Make another straight stitch, then another diagonal, repeating the process for as many stitches as you want.

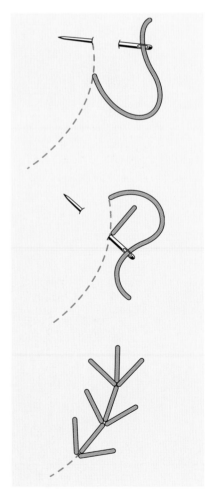

Daisy Stitch

Make two holes close together and a third hole about 1/8 inch (3 mm) across from them. Bring the needle up from the wrong side of the paper into the first hole. Bring the needle back down through the adjacent hole, leaving a loop of thread on the paper. Bring the needle back up through the third hole, then insert it into the loop that you left. Pull the thread until the loop rests against the paper, then bring your needle around the loop and down through the third hole. Continue with this process to make the next petal on the flower.

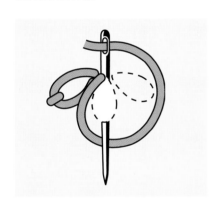

Satin Stitch

This stitch should only be used with strong paper, thin thread, small designs, and hand sewing. A machine-embroidered satin stitch will probably weigh down your paper too much, causing it to tear. A satin stitch is simply a series of closely placed straight stitches that fill in an outlined design. When doing a satin stitch on paper, it's a good idea to pencil in the outline of the design, so that your stitches align within the borders.

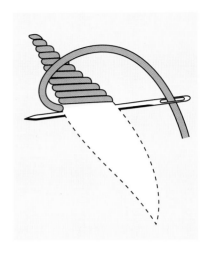

Chain Stitch

Mark the line you'd like to stitch on the paper. Use your piercing tool to make holes along the line where you want the finished stitches to be. Create additional holes about one-third of the distance from the first stitch holes. Insert the needle from the wrong side into the first hole. Pass the needle over the next hole and bring it down into the hole after that. Then bring the needle up through the hole you skipped to create the chain.

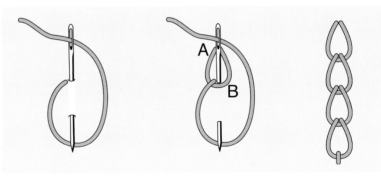

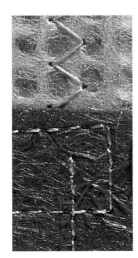

Family Tree

Sure to become a treasured heirloom, this family tree project can be framed or used as a scrapbook page. Use all your favorite small-pattern papers for the leaves so that the designs don't overwhelm the family names and dates you'll write on them.

You Will Need

Pencil

Templates on page 126

Tracing paper or scrap paper

Solid card stock

Scissors

Patterned and solid
    scrapbook or
    decorative papers

Masking tape

Sewing machine

Sewing thread in
    complementary colors

Pens with archival ink

Instructions

1 Tace the tree, leaf, and nest templates on page 126 onto tracing paper or copy them onto scrap paper, adjusting

the sizes to fit the card stock you'll use for the background. Cut them out in the patterned or solid papers of your choice. Cut out the bird and egg shapes freehand.

2 Attach the tree shape to the card stock, using small bits of masking tape. Machine stitch it to the card stock using a feather or other decorative stitch, then remove the pieces of masking tape. Repeat the process with the nest, egg, bird, and leaf pieces.

3 Add names and dates to the leaves with archival-ink pens.

DESIGNER
Nathalie Mornu

Stylish Storage Hatbox

Tiny mirrors stitched onto paper turn this storage piece
into a decorative accent. Use paper that complements
your décor and the decorative stitch of your choice.

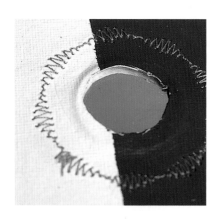

Instructions

1 On the back side of the
   paper, draw around the lid.
Add 1/2 inch (1.3 cm) all the way
around and cut.

2 Measure the side of the lid.
   Add 3/4 inch (1.9 cm) to the
width and 1/4 inch (6 mm) to the
diameter. If you can't get this size
piece from one piece, you can
cut it from two or more strips.
Cut this out.

3 Take the side and width
   measurements of the hatbox. Add 3/4 inch (1.9 cm) to the
width and 1/4 inch (6 mm) to the
diameter. If you don't have
enough paper to go all the way
around, you can piece it.

4 Glue each of the mirrors to
   a 1 1/2-square (3.8 cm)
piece of vellum.

5 Decide where you want the
   mirrors to go on the hatbox, and mark the spots with a
pencil. Place the 3/4-inch (1.9 cm)
mirror over the first spot. Cut
around the mirror with a craft
knife and repeat for each spot
where you want to place a mirror.

6 After you have cut all the
   circles, glue each vellum-
backed mirror to the back of the
paper. This will hold them in
place while you're stitching.

7 Practice machine stitching
   around the mirrors with
scrap paper and an extra mirror.
Find a decorative, zigzag, or
straight stitch that you like. You'll
find that you can line up the
presser foot next to the mirror
and just stitch around, keeping
the foot touching the mirror.
When you're comfortable with the
process, stitch the mirrors onto
the paper.

8 To glue the paper onto the
   hatbox, start on the lid. First
cut triangles out of the edges,
then wrap the paper around. The
edge will fold down easily
because of the cuts. Just keep
pressing down to make a crisp
edge on the top. Rub the whole
area to get any air bubbles out
and keep the paper flat.

9 To apply the paper to the inside of the lid, just glue the edge even with the top and fold the rest down. Keep pressing the edge down—you don't need any slits cut; it will fit nicely and stay in place.

10 For the bottom of the hatbox, glue the paper in place, leaving 1/2 inch (1.3 cm) at the top and 1/4 inch (6 mm) at the bottom. Overlap the side edges. Fold and glue the top and bottom edges. Be sure to rub out air bubbles and smooth everything down. If the hatbox has a string handle, remove it before you glue on the paper. Remember how the string was knotted in place. Poke through the paper in the spots where the string runs through the box. After gluing on the paper, run the string back through the box.

DESIGNER
Joan K. Morris

Party-Favor Holder

An elegant, grown-up version of a child's party-favor bag, this cone-shaped holder is designed to hang from the back of a guest's chair and hold anything from dried flowers to a take-home treat.

You Will Need

Sheet of metallic card stock, 8½ x 11 inches (21.6 x 27.9 cm)

Straight pin

Scrap paper

Large paper clips

Pencil

Scissors

Sheet of coordinating patterned paper

Embroidery needle

Metallic thread

Hole punch

36 inches (91.4 cm) of narrow satin ribbon

Glass beads in coordinating colors

Instructions

1 With the metallic card stock, practice rolling up the cone shape. When you find a shape you like, push a straight pin through all the layers where the point meets in the front so that you can remember the shape.

2 Open the metallic card stock and place a piece of scrap paper on top of it. Reroll the cone shape. Hold the shape in place with the paper clips. On the scrap paper, draw around the top of the cone shape, marking the edges. Open the cone and cut out the scrap paper as a pattern.

3 Use the scrap paper pattern to cut out the patterned paper that goes around the top of the cone so that you get the size of the opening right.

Cut the opposite side of the paper to give it a decorative edge. Position the patterned paper at the top edge of metallic card stock.

4 Hand-stitch a blanket stitch all the way around the top edge of the cone to join the metallic paper to the patterned paper.

5 Sew a straight stitch on the lower cone part of the metallic card stock, about ¼ inch (6 mm) in from the edge.

6 On the point where the pin was pushed through, punch two holes. Thread the ribbon onto the embroidery needle. Find where the pin went through to the inside of the cone and stitch the ribbon through all the layers and back down just through the first layer. Tie a knot in the ribbon and hide it behind the point.

7 At a point near the top of the cone where the pieces intersect, place a stitch or two with the metallic thread to hold the cone in place.

8 Stitch on the beads, starting from the back of the patterned paper and running the thread through the paper, the bead, the next bead (if you have more than one), and then back through the paper. Tie it off in the back.

9 At the top of the cone, punch one hole on each side. Tie one end of the remaining ribbon through one of the holes, then through the other and tie the other end.

DESIGNER
Joan K. Morris

Festive Flower Garland

For a special occasion or just to brighten up a room, a flower garland is a simple way to create a cheerful atmosphere. The flexible floral wire that forms the chain can easily be wrapped around a mantle, or held in place with tacks.

You Will Need

Pencil

3 sheets of mulberry paper, floral colors for the flowers, green for the leaves

Scissors

Small hole punch

Disappearing tape

Green thread

Sewing machine

Wire clippers

1 package of covered green floral wire in coordinating colors

Instructions

1 To make patterns for the flowers, start by drawing 2-inch-diameter (5.1 cm) circles on the mulberry paper. These will later become the flowers, so figure out how many flowers you want and draw that many circles. Draw 1^1/2 x 1^1/2-inch (3.8 x 3.8 cm) leaf shapes on the green paper, as many as you think you'll need for the leaves. At the bottom of each leaf, draw a small square to use as a tab to help join the flower and leaf together.

2 Cut the circles from the paper you want to use for the flowers. Cut the leaves from the green paper.

3 At the tip of each leaf, punch a ^{1}/8-inch-wide (3 mm) hole. Fold a piece of tape over both sides of the leaf. Punch out the hole again. This will strengthen the holes.

4 On each of the circles, draw a spiral to the center. Cut out the spiral.

5 Machine stitch a straight line starting with the tip of a leaf, and stitch through the center until you are 1 inch (2.5 cm) from the tab. Place one of the flower shapes so the tip of the spiral is tucked under the tab, then stitch over the tab. When you get to the center of the flower, lift the center out and stitch across, leaving the thread, and catch the other side. Position another leaf with the tab tacked under the previous leaf and stitch down. Repeat this on all the flowers.

6 Cut as many 6-inch (15.2 cm) lengths of floral wire as you'll need to connect all the flowers. Fold in the end of each wire $1/2$ inch (1.3 cm). Bend the wire a little to make it look more loose and natural.

7 Attach a cut piece of wire to one end of a leaf and pinch the wire shut. Place an alternate color flower at the other end of the wire. Repeat with all the flowers. Attach another wire at each end.

DESIGNER
Joan K. Morris

Paper Vase Slipcovers

An inexpensive bud vase can be given a makeover with a creative stitched paper "slipcover." The paper cover loosely follows the shape of the vase, creating a whole new form with a lot more style.

DESIGNER

Terry Taylor

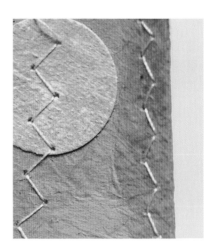

Instructions

1 Lay your vase on a piece of scrap paper. Trace around the shape of the vase. Don't be precise—you simply want the rough shape.

2 Fold the paper in half along the long axis of the vase.

3 Cut out the shape, just slightly outside the traced line. Unfold the paper. Use this symmetrical shape as a template.

4 Fan fold your handmade paper into four panels. Trace the template on the top fold. Cut out the shapes.

5 If desired, punch out a few small shapes with decorative punches, or cut them freehand.

6 Stitch the punched shapes to each of the four shapes.

7 Hold two shapes with the wrong sides together. Stitch along one edge. Add another shape, matching the edges and the wrong sides together. Add the fourth shape, aligning the edges, and stitch. Then align the last two edges and stitch them together.

8 Trim the thread ends. Slip the cover over the vase before you arrange the flowers.

Pastel Pennant Garland

As a temporary decoration for a party or a permanent addition to a nursery (or both!), this adorable string of pennants lends a festive feel to a room. This version is hand-stitched, but to save time, you could use a sewing machine with a decorative stitch.

You Will Need

- **9 sheets of assorted 8¹/₂ x 11-inch (21.6 x 27.9 cm) pastel-print papers**
- **Pencil**
- **Ruler**
- **Scissors**
- **Embroidery needle**
- **2 skeins of pearl cotton thread**
- **5 yards (4.57 m) of cotton clothesline, ¹/₂ inch (1.3 cm) thick**
- **Sewing machine**
- **Coordinating thread**

Instructions

1 Fold all nine pieces of paper in half (right side out) so they measure 8¹/₂ x 5¹/₂ inches (21.6 x 14 cm).

2 Find the center of one of the 5¹/₂-inch (14 cm) sides and lightly mark with a pencil. With the ruler, draw a line from each opposite corner to the center mark. This will make a triangle.

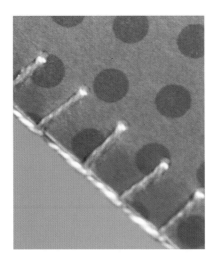

3 Cut out all the triangles. Leave each color together, right sides out, so each pennant is made from two pieces of paper with the same pattern.

4 With the pearl cotton thread, sew a blanket stitch ³/₄ inch (1.9 cm) down from the top edge, leaving the top open. Stitch all the way around and back up to ³/₄ inches (1.9 cm) from the top. Repeat for all the pennants.

5 Measure 4 feet (1.22 m) from one end of the clothesline. Place the clothesline inside the top opening of one of the pennants. Machine stitch on the top edge above the pennant. When the first pennant is done, skip 1 inch (2.5 cm) of the clothesline and move on to another pennant. Keep repeating this until you have stitched all of the pennants. Measure an additional 4 feet (1.22 m) of the clothesline and cut the end.

See the Light Curtain

Here's a lovely way to let soft light filter into a room without losing privacy. This curtain features gorgeous leaf-print paper that's a work of art in itself. You could just as easily use this piece as a wall hanging or hanging divider screen if you make it a little longer.

You Will Need

- 2 pieces 8½ x 11 inch (21.6 x 27.9) scrap card stock
- Pencil
- Scissors
- Ruler
- 16 sheets 8½ x 11-inch (21.66 x 27.9 cm) vellum
- Small paintbrush
- 16 sheets of 8½ x 11-inch (21.6 x 27.9 cm) handmade leaf-print paper
- Glue stick
- Sewing machine
- Jute thread
- Hole punch
- Jute string
- Bamboo stick, 36 inches (.91 m) long

Instructions

1 Fold the scrap card stock in half lengthwise and then in half again. Draw an arc on the open edge from corner to corner. Cut along the line. When you open it up, you'll have a nice oval shape. Repeat with the other piece of scrap card stock, but measure and make this one ¼ inch (6 mm) smaller.

2 Cut out 16 pieces of the larger pattern from the handmade paper. The edges will look too sharp, so, using the paintbrush and a bowl of water, paint the water on the edges of the paper and lightly tear the edges. You can just pick at the edges to give them texture.

3 Cut out 16 pieces of vellum using the smaller pattern as a guide.

4 Glue the vellum shapes to the back of the handmade paper shapes. Leave a ½-inch (1.3 cm) edge not glued. You don't want to stitch through glue.

5 With the velum side up, machine stitch around each piece, ¼ inch (6 mm) in from the edge to prevent the paper from wrinkling.

DESIGNER
Joan K. Morris

6   On a flat surface, lay the stitched pieces with the paper side up in an alternating pattern, four across and four down.

7   Punch holes in the appropriate places to tie them together and to the top.

8   Cut 24 pieces of jute string 10 inches (25.4 cm) long. Cut four pieces 16 inches (41 cm) long.

9   Using the 10-inch (25.4 cm) lengths of jute string, tie all the pieces together from top to bottom first, leaving 1 inch (2.5 cm) between each piece. Now tie all the pieces side to side. Tie them all with a square knot in the front. Later you can push the string to the back and tie another knot to the back.

10   At the top, run the jute through the punched holes and tie a knot at the length you want them, then tie a bow.

11   Slide the bamboo pole through the top knots.

Fashion Friends

Hang them in your laundry room or over your closet door. These adorable paper ensembles are just plain fun. Experiment with your favorite papers to come up with the perfect outfits, and embellish them to your heart's content.

DESIGNER
Joan K. Morris

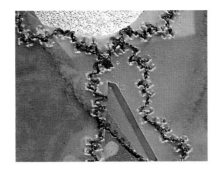

You Will Need

Pencil

Templates on page 125

Tracing paper

Scrap paper

Scissors

Glue stick

Assorted patterned papers

Assorted vellum

Metallic papers

Sewing machine

Matching thread

Small metallic beads

Gold metallic thread

String or yarn

Needle

Instructions

1 Trace the templates on page 125 onto tracing paper or look through fashion magazines to get ideas for the outfits. You can even trace a shape you like and make a few changes to the size and style.

2 On scrap paper, draw and cut out the design for each wardrobe element. If you're making a sweater or stole to add on top of a dress or skirt, cut the piece out separately. If you make a pleated skirt, draw a semicircle larger than the size you want the skirt to be.

3 Draw and cut out a pattern for the hanger (you'll need a back and a front piece). Place the hanger paper with wrong sides together and cut out the hanger shapes. Glue the two pieces of each hanger together.

4 To make a dress or blouse, cut two pieces of patterned paper with the wrong sides together. Place a hanger between the wrong sides of the wardrobe piece and glue in place.

5 Machine stitch a decorative pattern around the necklines, sides, and bottoms of the sleeves.

6 If you want to add metallic accents, such as the stitching on the gold dress, hand-stitch rows of stitches with metallic thread on one piece of the pattern before gluing on the back side. If you want to add beads, do the same.

7 To add pleats, practice folding on a scrap piece of paper to get the shape you want. Once you have the pleating figured out, pleat both sides of the skirt and a piece of vellum to go between the two sides. Glue the pieces together, then machine stitch across all of the pieces.

8 Slip a piece of string or yarn through the hangers when you're done.

Modern Life Lampshade

Reminiscent of the simple, space-age designs found
in mid-century fabrics and furniture, this cylindrical
lampshade makes a real style statement.

You Will Need

Ruler

Scissors

Large piece of light-
colored paper

Scrap paper

Purchased cylindrical
lampshade,
12 x 5 inches
(30.5 x 12.7 cm)

Pencil

Templates on page 125

3 pieces of blue metallic
card stock, each
8$\frac{1}{2}$ x 11 inches
(21.6 x 27.9 cm)

3 pieces of brown
metallic card stock,
each 8$\frac{1}{2}$ x 11 inches
(21.6 x 27.9 cm)

Hole punch

Sewing machine

Sewing thread

Glue stick

Clothespins

Instructions

1 Measure and cut a piece of
light-colored paper and a
piece of scrap paper to the exact
measurement of the lampshade.

2 On the cut piece of scrap
paper, draw the design,
using the template on page 125
as a guide. Start by measuring
out three equal spaces from side
to side. Measure 1 inch (2.5 cm)
down from the top and up from
the bottom and draw lines. Now
draw in the columns. They are
approximately 2$\frac{1}{2}$ inches (6.4
cm) wide at the top and bottom
and $\frac{1}{2}$ inch (1.3 cm) wide in the
center. Draw $\frac{1}{2}$-inch (1.3 cm)
columns at the ends. Draw the
oval shapes. Adjust the design as
necessary.

3 Cut the shapes from scrap
paper to use as patterns.

4 Cut out 1-inch-wide (2.5
cm) strips of blue card
stock for the bottom and the top
bands. Use the oval patterns to
cut ovals from the blue paper.

5 Cut out column and oval shapes from the brown card stock.

6 Draw the design for the center of the brown oval and punch holes at the end of each line.

7 Machine stitch the center-lines for the brown ovals. Place the brown ovals on the blue ovals and machine stitch them together close to the edge.

8 Position the designs on the off-white paper and glue them in place.

9 Machine stitch all the pieces close to the edges.

10 Glue the finished piece to the lampshade. Use clothespins to hold it in place until the glue dries.

DESIGNER
Joan K. Morris

Stitched Stockings

A great alternative to gift wrap, these stockings are easy to sew and sturdy enough to hold not only flat items, such as gift certificates, but also stocking stuffers of all kinds.

You Will Need

Pencil

Templates on page 123

Scrap card stock, 8½ x 11 inches (21.6 x 27.9 cm)

Scissors

12 sheets of 8½ x 11 inch (21.6 x 27.9 cm) card stock in assorted colors

Sewing machine

Embroidery needle

Sewing thread in holiday colors

2 skeins of cotton pearl embroidery floss in two different holiday colors

Instructions

1 Copy the stocking template onto a piece of scrap card stock and cut it out to use as a pattern. Trace the pattern onto a piece of colored card stock.

2 Copy the tree, holly leaf, and/or star templates in different sizes onto scrap card stock, cut them out, then trace them onto card stock in colors that contrast with the stocking color and cut them out. To make the holly berries, cut out small circles in the color of your choice (most likely red!).

3 Place the decorative designs on the stocking shape and machine stitch around the edges with a medium-length straight stitch, sewing as close as you can to the edge. You will need to stop the machine with the needle down and move the paper to make the curves and corners. On the stars, sew a smaller star shape in the middle, if you like.

4 When you have finished stitching around the decorative elements, trim the edges.

5 Blanket stitch the top edge of each stocking with the embroidery floss.

6 Place the front and the back pieces of each stocking together and blanket stitch all the way around the stocking, leaving the top open.

7 Stitch a braided piece of floss in a loop at the top left corner of the stocking to serve as a hanger.

DESIGNER
Joan K. Morris

Carnival Mask

For carnival, Mardi Gras, or a masked-ball theme party, there's no better way to express your creativity than with a handmade mask. Metallic thread really makes the design stand out. Use lots of ribbons for an extra festive touch.

You Will Need

Pencil

Template on page 126

Scrap paper

Scissors

1 sheet metallic card stock

Sewing machine

Metallic-colored sewing thread

Metallic thread

Craft knife

1 sheet of metallic vellum

1 roll of satin ribbon, 1/8 inch (3 mm) wide

1 roll of wire-edged ribbon, 1/2 inch (1.3 cm) wide

Hole punch

Instructions

1 Trace the mask template onto scrap paper, then draw and cut out the mask pattern.

2 Using the pattern, cut out the mask shape from the card stock.

3 Hold the shape up to your face and mark the position where the eyes should go. Draw the diamond designs on the mask in the positions of your choice.

4 To machine stitch the design, you'll use the regular gold thread in the bobbin and the metallic thread on top (metallic thread can be difficult to work with if you use it in the bobbin). The metallic thread will show up on top. At this point, it's a good idea to practice the zigzag stitching on a piece of scrap card stock. Just work slowly and stop the machine and turn the card as you go around curves. On the diamonds, you want to stitch well beyond the corner before you turn them. You'll see; just practice.

5 Cut out the inside of the diamonds with the craft knife. Be sure to keep away from the stitches. Leave the eyes in place.

(Instructions continue on page 40)

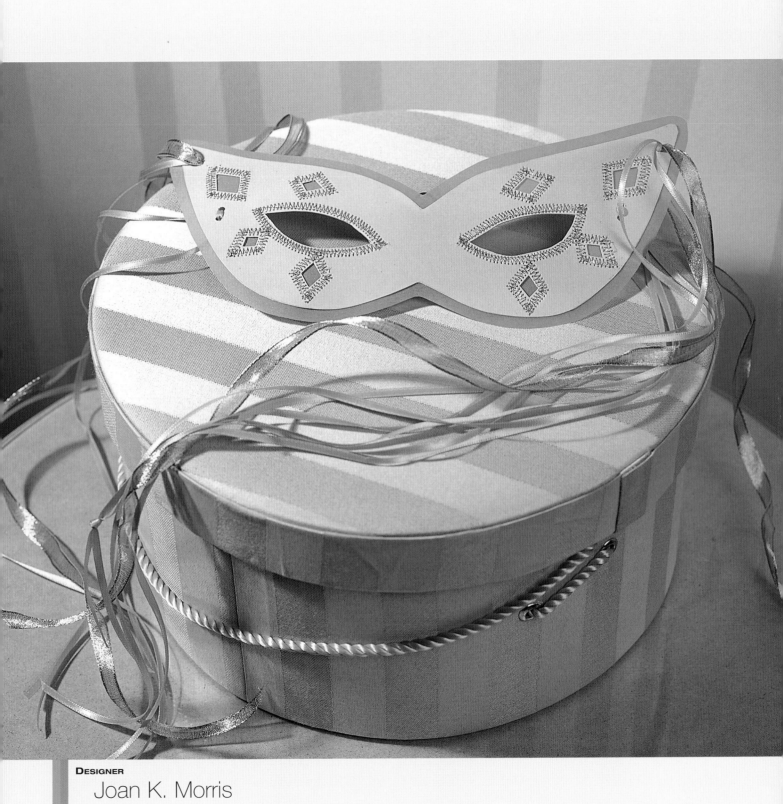

DESIGNER
Joan K. Morris

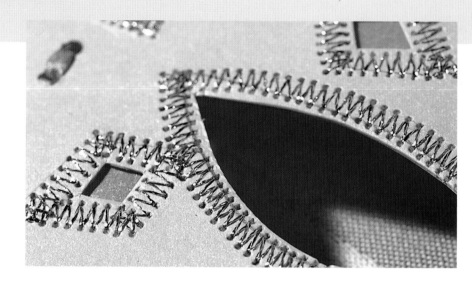

6 Glue the vellum to the back of the mask.

7 Cut around the mask, leaving a ¼-inch (6 mm) border of vellum.

8 Carefully cut out the eyes with the craft knife. You'll be cutting through the vellum and the card stock.

9 Cut six 36-inch (91.4 cm) lengths of satin ribbon.

10 Cut two 36-inch (91.4 cm) lengths of wire-edged ribbon.

11 Punch a hole in each upper corner of the mask. Punch two holes off to the side to the right of each eyehole, positioning one hole on top of the other.

12 For the ribbon tie, run a 36-inch (91.4 cm) length of satin ribbon through the hole to the side of each eye opening. Tie knots in the ends. These will be tied in back to hold on the mask.

13 Run two lengths of satin ribbon and one length of wire-edged ribbon halfway through each of the holes in the upper corners. Give the wire-edged ribbons a curl and let the satin ribbons hang.

Party Crown

Revelers young and old will love a custom-made crown to wear for a birthday party or other special occasion, or just for playing dress-up. This playful version features over-the-top gold glitz and flashy gems, but you could just as easily use elegant silver paper and little rhinestones or other silver-tone embellishments for a more demure headpiece. Using hook-and-loop tape for the closure makes the size adjustable.

DESIGNER
Joan K. Morris

41

Party Crown

- Pencil
- Ruler
- Scrap paper
- Scissors
- 3 sheets of 8½ x 11-inch (21.6 x 27.9 cm) metallic-color decorative paper
- 1 piece of card stock, 8½ x 11 inches (21.6 x 27.9 cm)
- Craft knife
- Paint pen in color that matches your paper
- Sewing machine
- Coordinating thread
- Glue stick
- White hook-and-loop tape (self-sticking)
- White craft glue
- Assorted plastic gems (flat backs)

Instructions

1 Draw your crown design on scrap paper using the 11-inch (27.9 cm) edge as the bottom. This will be the front of the crown—you will add the rest later. You don't want the crown to be much taller than 6 inches (15.2 cm). Draw circles for the jewels so you know where to place them. Cut out the crown and try it on to see whether it looks right.

2 Place two of the metallic papers together with the card stock in between. Make sure the metallic color is facing out on both pieces. Draw around the paper pattern. Cut out the pieces out together so there's no overlap, using scissors to cut the outer edges and a craft knife for the inside cuts.

3 With the paint pen, paint around all the edges, about ¼ inch (6 mm) in and on the very edge. This prevents any white paper from showing through. Let dry.

4 Place some gems on the front and cut out pieces of paper to get an idea of your design. Draw a zigzag line around the gems to machine stitch. Draw swirls that you'll later hand-stitch. You want to stitch these designs through the top layer only.

5 Machine stitch along the zigzag line you drew in step 4. Hand stitch a chain stitch for the swirls.

6 Cut the last piece of gold paper in half lengthwise. Fold both pieces lengthwise. You will have two pieces, each 2 x 11 inches (5.1 x 27.9 cm).

7 Glue the folded pieces shut with the glue stick, being careful not to place any glue at the edges, because you don't want to stitch through glue.

8 Glue the long pieces to the stitched crown with the glue stick, about 1 inch (2.5 cm) in from the sides. These pieces are the back of the crown.

9 Glue the inside card stock to the back of the crown with the glue stick, being careful not to place glue where you'll be stitching. Now glue the front to the back.

10 Machine stitch the bottom edge, the sides where the back attaches, the top edges of the long pieces, and the decoration on the top.

11 Try on the crown, and leave a 3-inch (7.6 cm) overlap in the back. Cut off the excess.

12 Place the self-sticking hook-and-loop tape under the overlap, positioning it so the size of the crown can be adjusted.

13 Lay out the gems on the crown. When you are pleased with the design, glue them in place with white craft glue.

Be My Guest Place Cards

Make your guests feel special with these easy-to-make, reusable place cards, designed to be held in simple clip place-card holders. The outer "envelope" portion slips into a clip, and the inner card is used for the guest's name. After you've written on the inner card, you can simply throw it out and use a different one for your next event.

You Will Need

- Ruler
- Scissors
- 2 sheets of metallic card stock
- Scrap paper
- Pencil
- Craft knife
- Hole punch
- Embroidery needle with large eye
- Skein of decorative yarn
- Contrasting metallic or other solid-color card stock

Instructions

1 For each place card, measure and cut out two pieces of metallic card stock in the first color, each 2$\frac{1}{2}$ x 4 inches (6.4 x 10.2 cm).

2 On scrap paper, draw and cut out an oval shape for the center of the place card. Draw this shape onto a piece of the cut card stock in the color you want to use for the envelope portion of the place card. Cut it out with the craft knife.

3 On the top edge of the card you just cut out, mark, and punch out five holes. The holes should be about $\frac{1}{4}$ inch (6 mm) apart all the way around the center.

4 Thread the embroidery needle with the yarn and stitch from hole to hole on the top, leaving extra yarn at each end to tie off the side pieces. Stitch around the center, back-stitching as you go to make sure the yarn covers. As the ends

meet, tie them in a knot. You can hide the knot later.

5 Place the stitched front over the piece of the card you'll use for the back. Mark holes along the side of the back piece and the bottom edge, about $\frac{1}{4}$ inch (6 mm) apart or closer. Align the front and back and punch holes through both pieces.

6 Start stitching at the top of one edge by tying the end of the yarn to the top piece of yarn; hide the knot inside. Wrap the yarn around the top edge and start stitching all the way around the sides and bottom, backstitching the whole way.

7 At the other end, tie the end of the yarn to the other piece and hide the knot inside.

8 Cut out a piece of card stock 3$\frac{1}{4}$ x 2 inches (8.3 x 5.1 cm) in a contrasting color for the inner piece on which you'll write the name.

Sweetheart Valentine Holder

Start a new family tradition. This heart-shaped holder is a charming way to store cherished valentines and can be used year after year. The handle makes it easy to carry to school or hang on a chair or doorknob.

Instructions

1 On scrap paper, draw a heart shape. To keep the shape proportionate, you can draw half of the heart, then fold the paper in half and cut it out.

2 On one piece of red card stock, draw around the heart pattern. Place the second piece of red card stock against the first one and cut out the two pieces together.

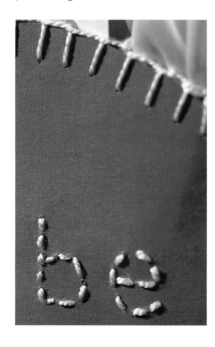

3 Using the pattern, cut out the two pieces of patterned paper for the lining. If the paper is one sided, be sure to cut it to the correct orientation so that the pattern faces out. Also, cut inside the cutting line, so that the lining paper is a little smaller than the card stock. Set the pieces aside.

4 On the scrap paper pattern, draw your letter placement. You can also draw the stitch placement.

5 You can use carbon paper to trace the letters onto the card stock, but the tracing may show up after you stitch. Another idea is to place the pattern over the card stock and, with a pin, poke the shape of the letters through both layers.

6 With the cotton pearl floss and the embroidery needle, stitch a running stitch starting at the top of the letter B. Just follow the piercing of the letters. Since you're going to add a layer of lining inside, don't worry about the knots and floss showing. To dot the I, make a French knot.

7 Position the heart buttons and stitch in place. If they seem to wobble, you can dab on some white craft glue to keep them from moving.

8 Glue the liner paper to the wrong side of each heart piece, placing the glue line $1/2$ inch (1.3 cm) in from the edges (this will make it easier to stitch).

9 Decide how big an opening you want to leave at the top. Before joining the two hearts together, sew a blanket stitch across the top edges of the hearts.

10 Measure out the length of ribbon you want for the handle and stitch it in place at the top of each heart. Glue the extra end of the ribbon to the inside of the heart.

11 Place the two hearts together, right sides out. At the spot you choose to start the opening, stitch from front to back, with the stitches almost on top of each other, to create a strong binding. Now start a blanket stitch and go all the way around the edge until you get to the opening. Stitch around at this point and knot the end, hiding the knot.

DESIGNER
Joan K. Morris

Autumn Wreath

Echoing the shapes and colors of the falling leaves, this autumn wreath is a great way to celebrate the season. A foam square serves as a base, but you could use a round one if you choose a different shape for your leaves or position them differently on the foam form.

You Will Need

Pinking shears

6 sheets of card stock in autumn colors

Thread in contrasting colors to the card stock

Sewing machine

Scissors

Foam square, 1 x 12 x 12 inches (2.5 x 30.5 x 30.5 cm)

Craft knife

Straight pins

Grosgrain ribbon for the foam form cover, 1¼ inches (3.2 cm) wide

80 color-tipped pins (Note: you can paint pinheads with nail polish if you can't find enough)

50 amber beads

12 faceted beads

Ruler

Marking pen

1 yard (91.4 cm) of wide grosgrain ribbon for hanger

1 yard (91.4 cm) of narrow, contrasting ribbon

Instructions

1 Using the pinking shears, cut about 30 leaf shapes out of one color of the card stock and 15 in a second color. Use contrasting thread to machine stitch a featherstitch on the leaf shapes.

2 On the wide end of a leaf, use the scissors to make a slightly curved cut about 1 inch (2.5 cm) long (avoid cutting any decorative stitching). To give the leaves dimension, lap one side of this cut over the other, hold in place with your fingers, and stitch. Repeat with all the leaves. Set aside.

3 If the foam square is solid, cut out its center with a craft knife, creating a 1-inch-wide (2.5 cm) frame. Use straight pins to attach the grosgrain ribbon to the inside and outer edges to cover the foam. Fold the excess width of ribbon over the same side of the frame. This will serve as the front once you start pinning the leaves to it.

4 Use straight pins to attach the leaves to the front side of the foam frame, alternating the colors of the leaves. Use as few pins as possible, and pin only the wide end of the leaves. If the end of the leaf hangs off the interior edge of the frame too far, you can simply fold it back. Try to hide the pins by overlapping the leaves as you keep working around the frame in the same direction. When you have space left for only one leaf, carefully work it in under the very first leaf you pinned down, then unobtrusively pin it into position.

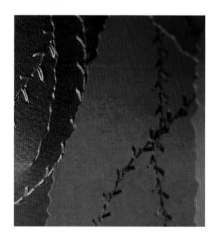

5 Replace any straight pins that remain visible with color-tipped pins.

6 Attach the amber and faceted beads in clusters, using the color-tipped pins.

7 Measure, mark, and cut slits in the wide grosgrain ribbon, perpendicular to its edges. The slits should be exactly the width of the narrower ribbon; make the first slit 1 inch (2.5 cm) away from one end of the ribbon. The next slit should be 4 inches (10.2 cm) from the first. Continue slitting along the length of the grosgrain, alternating the spaces between slits so they're 1 inch (2.5 cm), then 4 inches (10.2 cm), apart. Next, weave the narrow ribbon through the slits. To hang the wreath, attach the ribbon to the back of the frame using straight pins.

DESIGNER
Nathalie Mornu

49

Minilight Covers

Give plain minilights a makeover with little vellum shades that filter the light beautifully. The square shape keeps the vellum away from the bulb for safety.

You Will Need

(For 12 light covers:)

Ruler

Scissors

3 sheets of clear vellum, 12 x 12 inches (30.5 x 30.5 cm)

4 sheets of colored vellum

Sewing machine with zigzag stitch

Thread in coordinating colors

White craft glue

Small hole punch

Embroidery needle

Skein of embroidery floss

String of small, white, minilights

Craft knife

Cutting board or cardboard

Instructions

1 Cut all three 12 x 12-inch (30.5 x 30.5 cm) sheets of vellum into four 6 x 6-inch (15.2 x 15.2 cm) squares to create twelve 6-inch-square (15.2 x 15.2 m) shades.

2 Cut out a 2-inch (5.1 cm) square from each corner of each 6-inch (15.2 cm) square. You will have twelve square cross-shaped pieces.

3 From each of the four sheets of colored vellum, cut out twelve 1$\frac{1}{4}$-inch (3.2 cm) squares.

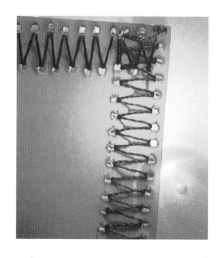

4 Practice making the zigzag stitch on the vellum. If you make the stitches too close together, the vellum will tear. Practice stitching the corners. Stop with the needle down, lift the presser foot, turn the vellum, lower the presser foot, and start down the other side. Once you've got it down, continue to the next step.

5 You'll have to decide whether you want the thread to match or contrast the color of the vellum. Zigzag stitch your first vellum square, then zigzag stitch a square in a different color on the opposite side. Change thread if necessary. At the end where the stitching meets, place a little dab of white glue to keep the zigzag stitching from raveling.

6 Punch a hole in the outer corner of each shade. Punch a hole in the center of each cross-shaped piece. Cut a line from one of the inside corners to the center punch.

7 Place the cross wrong side up, and fold and crease each flap over to the center.

8 Run embroidery floss from the front through the punched holes to the back and tie a knot. Trim close. Repeat with all the corners.

9 Slide each lightbulb through the top slit in each shade and into the center punched hole. The pressure of the vellum will hold them in place.

DESIGNER
Joan K. Morris

Scrap-Stash Cards

Use up all those little odds and ends of decorative paper you have stashed away. Gather several papers, solid and translucent, and then cut and punch out simple shapes. Thread your sewing machine with a complementary color and get busy.

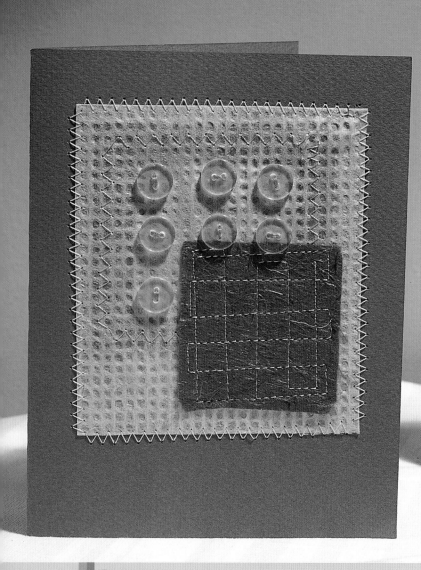

DESIGNER
Terry Taylor

Scissors

Solid, patterned, and translucent papers

Decorative-edge scissors

Decorative punches

Sticker machine

Sewing machine

Coordinating thread

Greeting cards or card stock

Buttons

Instructions

1 Cut out a large, simple shape in one of your papers.

2 Use decorative-edge scissors and/or decorative hole punches to cut or punch out similar but smaller shapes in other types of papers. Don't forget to use the negative shapes that you get when you use decorative punches.

3 Run all the shapes through the sticker machine.

4 Remove the backing on a couple of the smaller shapes. Position one or two of them on the large shape. Add decorative machine-stitching.

5 Adhere a few more shapes and stitch them.

6 Stitch the large shape to the card or folded card stock.

7 Hand-stitch buttons to the card, if you like.

8 If you want to hide the stitching on the inside of the card, cut a piece of paper slightly larger than your completed design. Run it through the sticker machine, and then adhere it behind your stitched design.

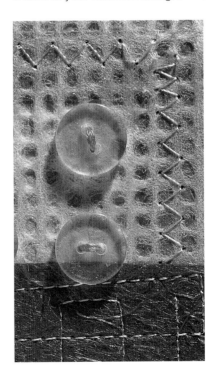

Paper Flower Cards

These easy-to-make cards are a great opportunity for a virtually mistake-free, beginning machine-stitching project. It's also a great way to use up some of those paper scraps in your stash. Vellum adds a fun element, because the paper shapes underneath can peek through.

You Will Need

Blank white card,
   5 x 7 inches
   (12.7 x 17.8 cm)

Punched-paper shapes
   in a variety of
   coordinating colors
   and textures

Sewing machine

Sewing thread

Scissors

Clear-drying craft glue

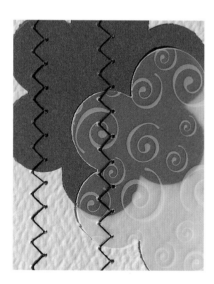

Instructions

1   Lay the card open with the front facing you. Lay out some punched-paper shapes on the surface until you find a design that appeals to you.

2   Carefully align the card so that the machine will begin stitching just off the surface of the card. Make sure the thread will move across your first paper shape.

3   Set the machine to your stitch of choice.

4   Begin running the machine, and very slowly move the card away from you. Because the paper shapes you've laid out have not been glued down, you may need to reposition them as you go. It's the carefree improvisational feel of this process that provides a sense of whimsy to the card. It's just fine, even advantageous, to have some of your shapes go off the surface of the card. This adds an interesting composition. You will simply cut off the excess in a later step.

5   You can work across the surface of the card in a straight line, or gently twist the card as it moves under the needle to create a delicate curve.

6   Don't stop until the thread has been sewn completely off the edge of the card.

7   Cut off any part of the paper shapes that may be left hanging off the edge of the card.

8   Cut off the excess thread at the top and bottom of the card. Apply a small dot of glue along each thread end on the inside cover of the card. This will dry clear and hold the thread ends in place. Set aside to dry.

Mesh Scrapbook Page

The addition of a mesh layer echoes the stitches used on this page, so that the mesh appears to be stitching, too. It's an interesting approach that can be used for lots of different layouts.

You Will Need

- Scrapbook paper
- Photo
- Decorative paper
- Scissors
- Sewing machine
- Coordinating sewing thread
- Clear plastic mesh
- Glue dots or other adhesive
- Glue gun and glue sticks
- Printer
- 1 sheet of vellum
- Twig
- Chalk
- Paper-piercing tool

Instructions

1 Select a background scrapbook page that coordinates with the dominant color in your photo for the page.

2 Choose a decorative paper in a coordinating color to serve as a photo mat and cut it the correct size for your photo. Machine-stitch it onto the scrapbook page using a straight basting stitch.

3 Adhere a sheet of clear plastic mesh on top of the photo mat with glue dots or other adhesive.

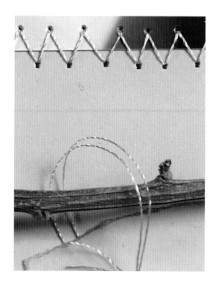

4 Sew your photo onto the smaller piece of decorative paper used as a mat using a zigzag stitch and coordinating thread.

5 Adhere a twig onto the small photo mat with a few dots of hot glue.

6 Print the words you want to use onto the vellum, then tear it into the desired shape. Chalk the edges of the vellum.

7 Using a paper-piercing tool, make three holes in the top of the title block.

8 Finish by hanging the title block from the twig using a double strand of thread.

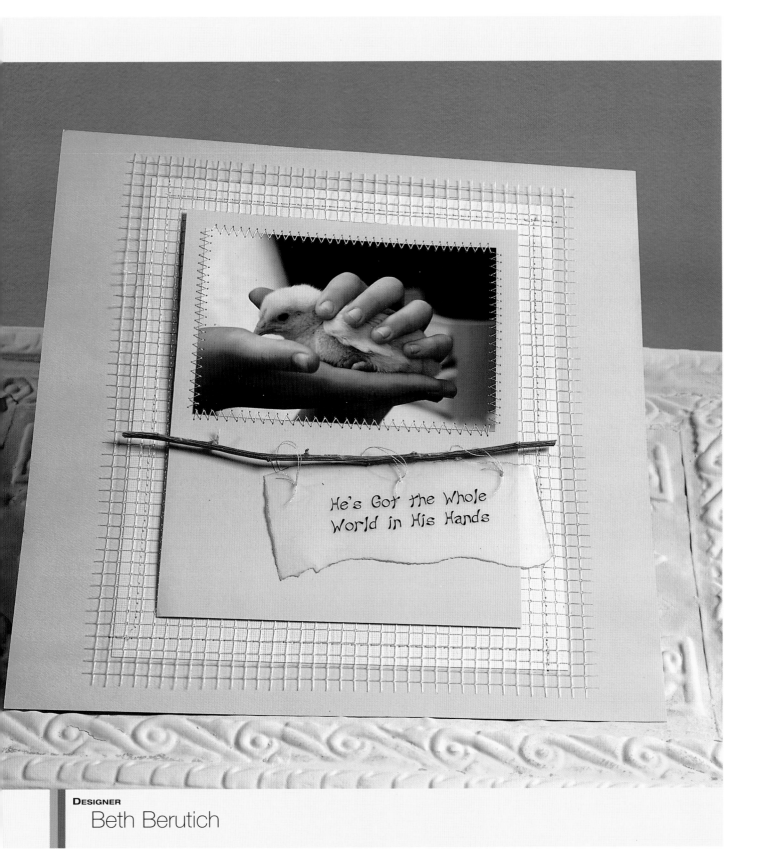

He's Got the Whole World in His Hands

DESIGNER
Beth Berutich

Sisters Scrapbook Page

Here's a cute idea for a scrapbook page. The layers and stitching give the page dimension, and the sunny design echoes the cheerful feel of the photograph.

You Will Need

- Scissors
- Card stock for photo mat
- Photo of your choice
- Archival glue
- Scrapbook paper
- Decorative papers or scrapbook paper in solid colors
- Sewing machine
- Sewing thread in several colors
- Piece of craft felt, 8½ X 11 inches (21.6 x 27.9 cm)
- Pencil
- Embroidery needle
- Embroidery floss
- Hole punch
- Micro-fiber yarrn

Instructions

1. Cut a piece of card stock to serve as a frame for your photo.

2. Adhere your photo on the mat with archival glue, then mount the mat on a piece of 8½ x 11-inch (21.6 x 27.9 cm) scrapbook paper.

3. Tear paper to form the stem, leaves, and flower petals in decorative papers that complement the photo.

4. Machine stitch the stems and leaves to the background paper with a zigzag stitch and light green thread.

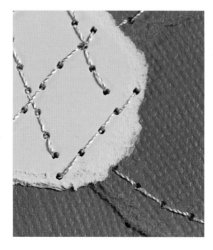

5. Use a straight basting stitch with light green thread to make veins in each leaf. Layer on leaves in two colors of green for dimension, edges extending (freely, not secured) off the background paper.

6. Sew on flower petals one at a time, layering each petal on top of the previous one, using white thread.

7. Using a zigzag stitch with yellow and gold thread, create a pattern for the inside of the flower.

8. Fold up the edges of the leaves and the flower petals so they pop off the page.

9. Adhere the background paper to the craft felt.

10. Adhere the felt to the colored scrapbook paper.

11. Tear two layers of green paper to create grass at the bottom of the page.

12 Use light green thread to baste random grass onto the page.

13 Finally, sketch the word "Sisters" in pencil at the bottom left-hand side.

14 Use a hole punch to make holes for the large-eye needle to pass through.

15 Combine two colors of embroidery floss and one color of micro-fiber yarn to stitch the letters. Knot off in the background.

16 Attach a second large piece of scrapbook paper to the back of the first one to cover the stitches.

DESIGNER
Beth Berutich

Old-Fashioned Scrapbook Page

Dad may not have been born at the turn of the 20th century, but you can create that look if you like. Make the image even more vintage with a cross-stitched frame around the portrait. This particular profile was hand-cut by an old-fashioned silhouette portraitist during a family vacation.

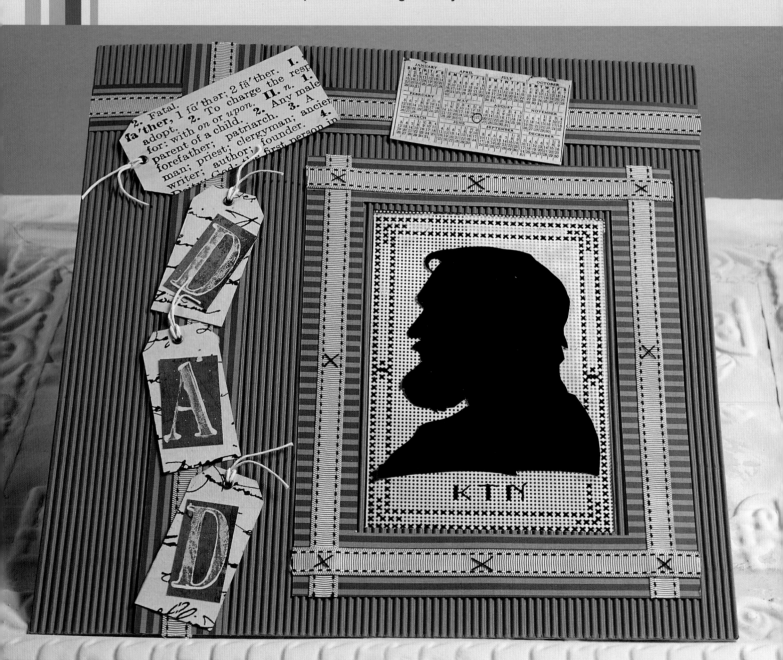

DESIGNER
Terry Taylor

You Will Need

- Copier
- Photograph in profile
- Black marker
- Stapler
- Black paper
- Sharp, pointed scissors
- Perforated paper*
- Pencil
- Embroidery thread
- Sharp needle
- Craft glue
- Craft knife
- Metal-edge ruler
- Corrugated paper
- Double-sided tape
- Decorative papers
- Tags
- Printed embellishments
- Sticker machine
- Stitched ribbon

*You can find this paper in the stitchery section of most craft stores.

Instructions

1 Enlarge and photocopy the photograph. Use the marker to outline the profile on the photocopy.

2 Reduce the photocopy as desired. Staple the photocopy to black paper. Use the sharp scissors to cut out the silhouette carefully. Set it aside.

3 Cut a piece of perforated paper slightly larger than the profile. Place the profile on the paper.

4 Lightly mark the paper around the edges where you'd like to make a line of cross-stitches to frame the profile.

5 Make a line of slanting stitches, then go back over the line and slant the stitches in the opposite direction.

6 When you have stitched a border you like, glue the profile to the paper.

7 Use a sharp craft knife and a metal-edge ruler to cut out an opening in the corrugated paper slightly smaller than the framed profile. Use double-sided tape to adhere the perforated paper to the back of the corrugated paper.

8 Cut decorative papers, tags, and embellishments as desired. Run them through the sticker machine. Set them aside.

9 Cut two long strips of decorative paper to the width of your page. Cut four shorter strips to frame the opening. Run them through the sticker machine.

10 Cut lengths of stitched ribbon to match the strips in step 9. Run them through the sticker machine, and then adhere them to the strips. If desired, add cross-stitches to the ribbon.

11 Frame the opening with the strips. Add the longer strips as desired on the page. Then add the tags and other decorative embellishments.

Tic-Tac-Toe Card

This cute card serves double duty: as a memorable greeting card and a three-dimensional tic-tac-toe board. Kids and grown-ups alike will love to display it and challenge others to a game of tic tac toe during downtime at the office or on long trips in the car.

You Will Need

Purchased blank card or folded piece of heavy paper

Pencil

Ruler

Sheet of clear vellum

Sewing machine

Sewing thread

Scissors

Templates on page 124

Colored construction paper

Instructions

1 Measure out and lightly mark the playing grid on the front of the card with a pencil and a ruler.

2 Cut three strips of vellum for the pockets so that their length is flush with the edges of the card. The bottom piece will fold under to the inside of the card, so it needs to be twice as wide as the other two.

3 Position the pockets where you want them on the card and machine sew the vertical lines with a straight stitch, following the grid you drew in step 1. Next, sew the horizontal lines across, also using a straight stitch. Tip: You can tie off the thread at the end of each row inside the card, using neat knots.

4 Trace the X and O templates on page 124 onto the construction paper and cut them out. Place the Xs and Os in the pockets.

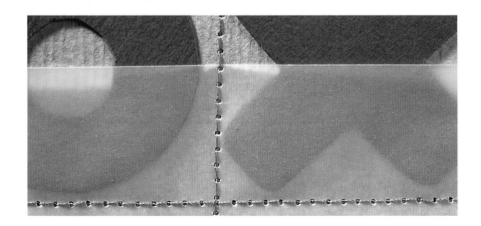

DESIGNER
Kristi Pfeffer

Days Gone By Memory Album

Use the cover of this little album to showcase a favorite family photo. Thin sheets of mica and a leather frame give the album an air of elegance.

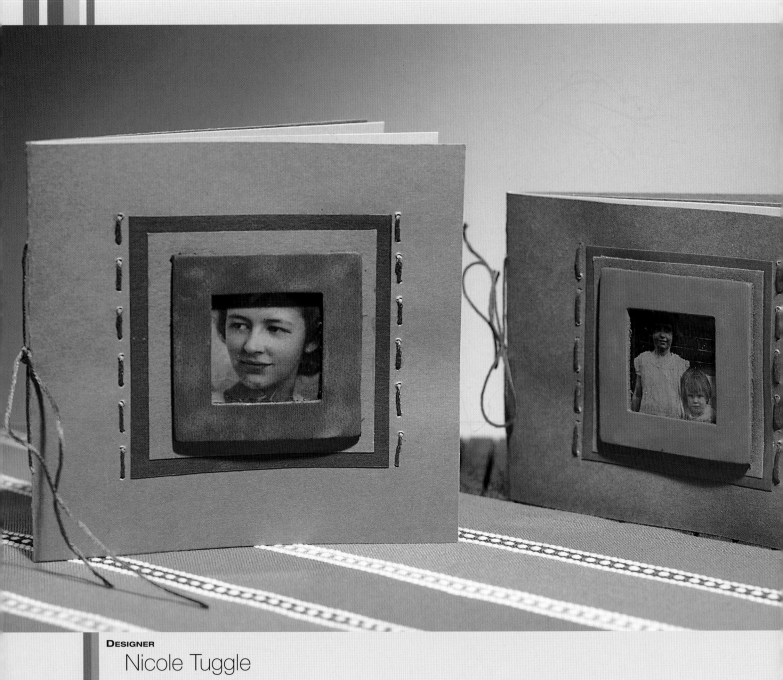

DESIGNER
Nicole Tuggle

You Will Need

3 sheets of decorative paper, each 4$\frac{1}{4}$ x 11 inches (10.8 x 27.9 cm)

Bone folder

Pencil

Ruler

Awl

Embroidery needle

Embroidery floss, 36 inch (70 cm) length

Scissors

Craft brush

Clear-drying craft glue

Decorative paper, 3$\frac{1}{4}$ inches (8.3 cm) square in same color as the embroidery floss

Decorative paper, 2$\frac{3}{4}$ inches (7 cm) square in same color as the card paper

Color copy of a black and white photo, 2 x 2 inches (5.1 cm) square

(Note: Color copies are sturdier than black and white photocopies and can be made sepia toned.)

Matte medium

Thin mica tile, 2 inches (5.1 cm) square

Leather frame, 2$\frac{5}{8}$ inches (6.7 cm) square

Instructions

1 To make the inside of the album, fold the three pieces of 4$\frac{1}{4}$ x 11-inch (10.8 x 27.9 cm) decorative paper in half to form 4$\frac{1}{4}$ x 5$\frac{1}{2}$ inch (10.8 x 14 cm) pages. Take care to match the corners exactly; hold the edges together with one hand and press down along the crease with a bone folder.

2 Stack the folded sheets together, one inside the next.

3 Open the stack of paper, folded edge facing down. Mark the center point of the fold lightly with a pencil. Mark 1 inch (2.5 cm) from the center point on each side.

4 Holding all the layers together, carefully poke through each pencil mark with an awl. Be sure to go through all the sheets of paper.

5 Thread the embroidery floss through the holes, starting from the outside of the card. Sew through the center hole, leaving a tail of thread long enough to tie a bow later. Sew up to the top hole, through the bottom holes, and back through the center hole where you started. Tie the thread in a bow and cut off the excess.

6 To embellish the cover, brush a thin layer of glue along the back of the 3$\frac{1}{4}$ inch-paper square (8.3 cm). Press onto the center of the cover.

7 Brush a thin layer of glue along the back of the 2$\frac{3}{4}$-inch paper square (7 cm). Press onto the center of the first paper square.

8 Brush a thin layer of glue along the back of the photo, and press onto the center of the paper squares. Set aside to dry.

(Instructions continued on page 66)

Days Gone By Memory Album

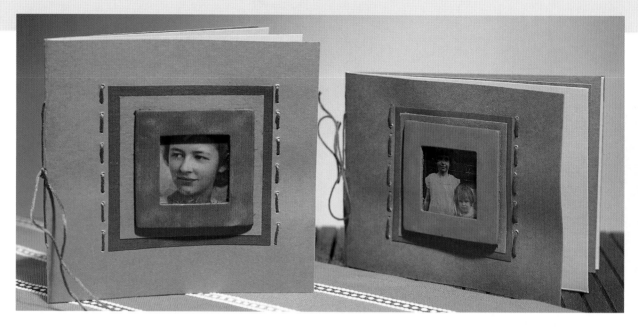

9 Brush a very thin, barely visible layer of matte medium onto one side of the mica tile. Press down onto the photo, taking care to push out any air bubbles. Set aside to dry.

10 Apply glue to the back of the leather frame, then carefully line it up over the photo and press down. Set aside to dry.

11 Mark with a pencil approximately $1/8$ inch (3 mm) to the right of the paper squares. Poke a hole through the pencil mark with the awl. Measure $1/2$ inch (1.3 cm) up from that first hole and poke another hole. Measure up $1/4$ inch (6 mm) and poke another hole. Measure $1/2$ inch (1.3 cm) from that and poke another hole. Repeat this until there are holes going up the entire side of the paper squares. Now, guide the threaded needle through the cover, starting from the inside and leaving a knot. Guide the needle back through the second hole. Sew in a running stitch until the last hole has been filled and the needle is coming through the inside of the album. Knot the end and tie off the excess. Repeat on the left side.

Accordion Frame

A sweet, simple, and inexpensive way to display your favorite photos, this is a great project for beginners. It might even be fun for kids and parents to make together.

DESIGNER
Emma Pearson

Accordion Frame

You Will Need

Pencil

Ruler

Card stock or
    construction paper

Craft knife

Eraser

Sewing machine

Coordinating thread

Paper clips

Instructions

1 Mark the measurements for the frame on your paper, keeping in mind that it will be folded in half.

2 Fold the paper in half, then unfold it again. Next, accordion fold the paper into sections of equal width (see figure 1).

3 Measure and draw a square in the center of each section on one half of the paper. Use a craft knife and a metal ruler to cut out the area inside the square you drew (see figure 2).

4 Refold the frame. The fold will become the bottom of your frame and you'll leave the top open so that you can slide the photos in when you're done.

5 Mark a line ½ inch (1.3 cm) in from the edge on each section of the frame to indicate where you'll sew the border. Unfold the frame again (see figure 3).

6 Choose your decorative stitch. With the frame unfolded, stitch across the top line of each section (that way, you'll still have a decorative stitch, but the front and back won't be sewn together, which would make it impossible to slip the photo in). When you're done with the top lines, refold the frame.

7 Fold up the frame and secure it in place with paper clips.

8 Back stitch a little before you start your decorative stitch. This will help secure the threads. Then sew the remaining three sides around each photo frame, meeting up with the top line.

9 Insert your photos through the top of the frame.

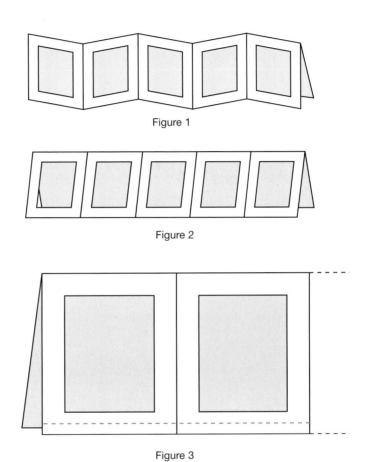

Figure 1

Figure 2

Figure 3

Country Chic Desk Set

An easy and inexpensive way to add elegance to an office, this desk set can be made from coordinating patterns of your favorite scrapbook papers. The rest of the materials—including the clock kit—can be found at craft stores.

You Will Need

Scissors

Ruler

6 sheets of scrapbook paper in assorted floral designs

1 sheet of white paper, 18 x 24 inches (45.7 x 61 cm)

Pencil

Glue stick

Sewing machine

Scrap paper

Thread in coordinating color

1 piece of cardboard, 16 x 22 inches (40.6 x 55.9 cm)

Juice can for penholder

Papier mâché box, 3 inches (7.6 cm) square

Awl

Purchased clock kit

3 x 8-inch (7.6 x 20.3 cm) piece of foam core, 1/4 inch thick (6 mm)

Craft knife

Instructions

1 Measure and cut the scrapbook paper into squares and rectangles of different sizes, ranging from 6-inch (15.2 cm) squares to 2 x 6-inch (5.1 x 15.2 cm) rectangles, and 2 x 8-inch (5.1 x 20.3 cm) rectangles.

2 On the 18 x 24-inch (45.7 x 61 cm) piece of white paper, draw a line 1/4 inch (6 mm) in from the edge all the way around. This gives you the border needed to arrange the papers.

3 Arrange the cut shapes on the large paper, stopping at the line you drew in step 2. Keep rearranging until you are pleased with the design. Overlap the edges of the papers 1/4 inch (6 mm) or more. Try not to put pieces of the same pattern next to each other. Save the leftover pieces.

4 When you are pleased with the design, lightly glue the design onto the large piece of paper with the glue stick.

5 Practice machine stitching on a scrap piece of paper to find the decorative stitch you want to use. If you don't have decorative stitches on your machine, you can use a straight stitch or zigzag stitch.

6 Since you'll be using a very large piece of paper, it's best to stitch in a straight line and not turn corners to stitch around the squares. Just start at the top and stitch down one edge, then, without cutting the thread, lift the needle and presser and move over to the next closest parallel edge. Do this all the way across one edge, until you have all the vertical lines. As you move over you will need to roll the paper toward the inside of the machine.

(Instructions continue on page 72)

DESIGNER
Joan K. Morris

Country Chic Desk Set

7 Next, stitch all the lines in the other direction. After you have finished all the lines, come back and trim the extra thread.

8 With the glue stick, attach the back of the stitched paper to the cardboard, making sure you center the cardboard so there is an even overlap. Fold the edges over to the back and glue in place. You can cut the corners at an angle to make a better fit.

9 For the pencil holder, take some of the leftover pieces and stitch it in rows, overlapping the edges by $^1/_4$ inch (6 mm). Make the total measurement $^1/_4$ inch (6 mm) taller then the juice can and $^1/_4$ inch (6 mm) wider. Place a row of stitches at the upper edge and where the sides will meet.

10 Glue the stitched paper onto the juice can, with $^1/_4$ inch (6 mm) at the top. Fold the top edge over to the inside and glue in place.

11 For the clock, pick two colors of paper, one for the lid (the face of the clock) and one for the box.

12 For the papier-mâché box, cut the floral paper so that it will cover the bottom and up the sides, and fold $^1/_4$ inch (6 mm) to the inside. On the corners you can fold it like a gift or cut off the layers. Glue in place.

13 For the clock face, poke a hole with an awl through the center of the lid large enough for the clock stem to come through (following the manufacturer's instructions).

14 Place the paper over the clock face and poke a hole through the same hole. Fold the paper over the edges to mark the size of the face. Either draw around a glass for the circle of the clock face or draw it freehand.

15 Machine stitch around the circle, using a decorative or straight stitch. Zigzag stitch at the 3:00, 6:00, 9:00, and 12:00 positions. Glue the stitched paper to the lid, making sure you center the clock face. Wrap the paper to the inside.

16 Insert the clock mechanism following manufacturer's instructions.

17 For the letter holder, cut the piece of foam core with a craft knife so that it measures 3 x 7 inches (7.6 x 17.8 cm). Measure from each 3-inch (7.6 cm) edge down $2\frac{1}{2}$ inches (6.4 cm) and draw a line. This will leave a 2-inch (5.1 cm) center. Using the craft knife, slice down through one side of the foam only, leaving one side uncut.

18 Fold up along the lines you have cut—this will create the U shape. To hold that position, you need to cut two very thin strips of the leftover foam core and glue them in place under each side edge.

19 Roughly measure all the way around the letter holder. Stitch together strips of paper, longer than that measurement by $3\frac{1}{2}$ inches (8.9 cm). After you have stitched the paper together, wrap the stitched paper around the letter holder and let the ends meet on the inside. Cut the ends to overlap by $\frac{1}{4}$ inch (6 mm). Fold the edges over to the outside edges.

20 Remove the paper and glue in place. The edges will not stay in place at first, so turn the letter holder on its side and lay a book on the top until the glue dries.

Bird-Watcher's Calendar

Even in the coldest winter months, these delightful birds will bring a touch of springtime to your day. To make it easier to sew with the metallic thread, use the pre-piercing method (see page 13) to create holes in advance.

You Will Need

- Pencil
- Bird and leaf templates on page 121
- Scrap paper
- Scissors
- Vellum in assorted pastel colors
- Purchased or handmade calendar
- 2 sheets of white card stock
- Metallic thread
- Embroidery needle
- Glue stick
- Sewing needle
- Sewing thread in coordinating colors
- Black embroidery floss
- Satin ribbon, 24 inches (61 cm) long
- Pre-glued picture hanger
- Hole punch

Instructions

1 Trace the bird template on page 121 onto scrap paper and cut them out.

2 Using the scrap paper patterns, cut out the birds from the vellum.

3 Trace the leaf template on page 121 onto scrap paper, then use it as a guide to cut out ten leaves from vellum.

4 Make your calendar on small sheets of paper, or use a purchased calendar.

5 Position the calendar on a piece of white card stock to help you decide where the birds and branches will go.

6 Position the birds on the card stock, but don't attach them yet. Lightly draw the branches around them. Remove the calendar and the birds.

7 With the metallic thread and the embroidery needle, stitch along the stem lines you drew using the stem stitch.

8 Glue the birds in place, then hand-stitch them in place with the coordinating thread, adding details to the wings, tail, legs, and beak area. Make the eyes using a French knot and the black embroidery floss.

9 Glue the leaves in place and add a straight stitch down the middle of each for detail.

10 Straight stitch a border all the way around the edge, about ¼ inch (6 mm) in, using the metallic thread.

11 Punch or poke two holes through the calendar and the stitched card stock, and run the satin ribbon through both pieces from the back to the front. Tie a bow and trim the ends of the ribbon, if necessary.

12 Glue the back of the stitched piece onto the other piece of card stock.

13 Place a picture hanger near the top of the back of the card stock.

DESIGNER
Joan K. Morris

Special Delivery Bracelet

The charming stitching on this cuff disguises its utilitarian roots: It's made from Tyvek, the specialty woven paper used for overnight delivery envelopes and home construction. It's durable but easy to work with, making it the perfect paper for all sorts of creative projects.

You Will Need

Ruler

Scissors

Tyvek envelope 10 x 13 inches (25.4 x 33 cm)

Sewing machine

Colored sewing thread

White sewing thread

Needle

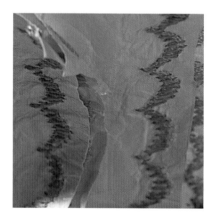

Instructions

1 Cut 15 rectangles from a Tyvek envelope, each 1³/₄ x 2 inches (4.4 x 5.1 cm). Crinkle them up for texture.

2 Machine stitch along the short edge of each rectangle with a decorative stitch in the thread color of your choice.

3 Use white thread for the remaining stitching. Cut a 3 x 9-inch (7.6 x 22.9 cm) strip of Tyvek. Crinkle it up. Turn each long edge under ¹/₄ inch (6 mm), then again another ¹/₄ inch (6 mm), and stitch with a straight stitch.

4 Fold the 15 rectangles in half widthwise, and crease a line with your fingernail to mark the line you'll stitch along. Measure 1 inch (2.5 cm) away from one short edge of the band, and place the centerline of a rectangle at this mark, perpendicular to the band's long edge. Hold in place with your fingers and stitch. Place the centerline of the next rectangle parallel to the centerline of the first one, ¹/₂ inch (1.3 cm) away on the band. Hold in place with your fingers and stitch. Repeat with the remaining rectangles.

5 Align the edges and stitch the band closed. Press the rectangles with finger pressure so they all face the same direction. Thread the needle, and spot stitch the rectangles so they don't flop around, but instead lay flat against the band.

Pretty Wall Pocket

There never seems to be enough space on your desk for all your papers and letters. Why not try the wall? This wall pocket gives you the extra space you need to get organized, and it's a great way to add a little color and pattern to a plain office wall.

You Will Need

4 pieces of patterned card
 stock, 6 x 9 inches
 (15.2 x 22.9 cm)

Sewing machine

Thread in two
 coordinating colors

Ruler

Scissors

2 pieces of card stock in
 a contrasting pattern,
 6 x 9 inches
 (15.2 x 22.9 cm)

Template on page 121

Piece of foam core,
 10 x 16 inches
 (25.4 x 40.6 cm)

Glue stick

2 pre-glued picture
 hangers

Instructions

1 Machine stitch the four pieces of card stock in the same pattern together with a $1/2$-inch (1.3 cm) overlap so that the paper measures 11 x 17 inches (27.9 x 43.2 cm).

2 Machine stitch rows lengthwise from top to bottom on the background paper, spacing the rows 1 inch (2.5 cm) apart.

3 Cut out the contrasting card stock to the size you need for the pockets.

4 Machine stitch rows of straight stitches across the contrasting cardstock every $1^{1}/2$ inches (3.8 cm). Machine stitch a decorative stitch $1/2$ inch (1.3 cm) down from the top of each row.

5 Fold the two pieces of pocket paper to make the pockets, using the pocket template on page 121 as a guide. Place them on the background paper, the first 1 inch (2.5 cm) from the bottom and the other 2 inches (5.1 cm) from the top. Machine stitch the sides and bottom edges.

6 Center and glue the paper to the foam core. Fold the edges over to the back. Add glue, if needed, to keep the edges down.

7 Place the picture hangers evenly on the upper back of the board.

DESIGNER
Joan K. Morris

Save Your Money Wallet

Making a wallet out of a recycled greeting card leaves you more money to put in it! This basic form can hold cash or credit cards and features a simple hook-and-loop tape closure to keep everything inside secure.

You Will Need

- Patterned greeting cards
- Ruler
- Scissors
- Hole punch
- Card stock in two colors of your choice
- Sewing machine
- Coordinating thread
- Masking tape
- Craft knife
- 7 inches (17.8 cm) of grosgrain ribbon, 1 inch (2.5 cm) wide
- Iron and ironing board
- 1 inch (2.5 cm) of hook-and-loop tape, ³/₄ inch (1.9 cm) wide

Instructions

1 Use the pattern on the greeting card as the front of the wallet. Decide what size you want it to be so that it will fit inside a pocket or purse. Measure and cut the card to the size you want for your wallet. Cover any printing (brand name, price, etc.) by sewing a strip of a second card or a different part of the pattern over it. Trim the edges.

2 Punch some holes in one color of card stock. Place the punched-out circles on the card and machine stitch over them with a decorative stitch to attach them to the card in a random pattern.

3 Place the card face up on the second color of card stock and attach the two together with masking tape. Trim the card stock so that it's about ¹/₄ inch (6 mm) smaller than the card.

4 Fold the grosgrain ribbon in half, press with the iron, and hand-stitch the fuzzy piece of the hook-and-loop tape on the grosgrain, facing out of the fold, but close to it. Stitch along both long exterior edges of the grosgrain to close the double layer of ribbon. Press the open edge under; determine where to attach it to the wallet, then stitch it down. Determine where to attach the hook side of the hook-and-loop tape on the opposite side of the wallet, then stitch it down.

5 For the inside of the wallet, cut a piece of card stock the same length as the card, but ¹/₂ inch (1.3 cm) narrower than its width. Create the credit card/ID

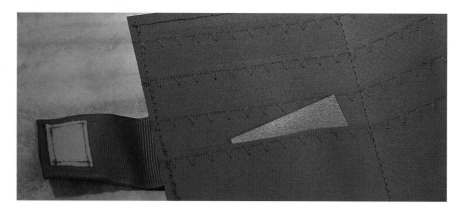

slots by cutting three pieces of card stock, each as long as the front card and 2 1/8 inches (5.4 cm) wide. Stitch decoratively along one long edge of each of these three pieces. Using mask-ing tape, lightly attach the pieces to each other, overlapping them by 3/4 inch (1.9 cm). Measure and mark the vertical center line of the three pieces (what will even-tually be the fold), and stitch it.

6 Tape the layers of the wal-let together, then stitch 1/8 inch (3 mm) from the outer edge of the wallet's face. Trim all edges evenly to the wallet's face using a ruler and a craft knife.

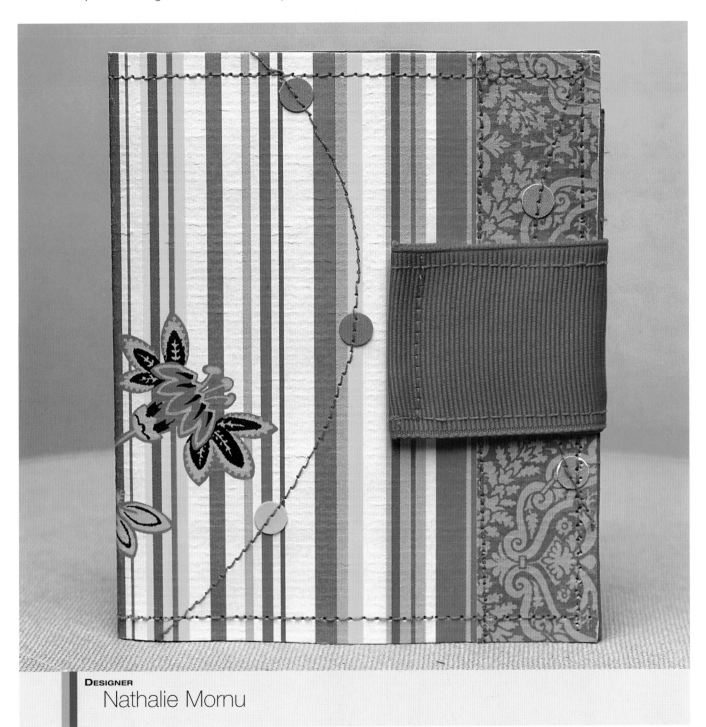

DESIGNER
Nathalie Mornu

Classic Bookmark

In the past, books came with their own ribbon bookmarks, sewn right into the bindings. This updated design lets you play with fanciful stitches while paying homage to the old tradition with a sewn-in ribbon tail.

You Will Need

- 1 sheet of vellum
- Printer or copier machine
- Scissors
- Ruler
- Pencil
- Card stock in two different patterns
- Craft knife
- Masking tape
- 1½ inch wide (3.8 cm) satin ribbon
- Thread
- Sewing machine

Instructions

1 Choose a literary saying for the bookmark and transfer it to a sheet of vellum by printing or photocopying it onto the vellum. Cut it out with scissors, leaving space around it for sewing it into the bookmark later.

2 Measure, mark, and cut a 1³/₁₆ x 8-inch (3 x 20.3 cm) piece out of the card stock you'd like to use for the front of the bookmark. Determine how big of a window you'll need for your printed saying. On the wrong side of this piece of card stock, measure and mark the window. Cut out the window with the craft knife, using the ruler to keep the lines perfectly straight. Be careful not to extend your cuts past the corner lines of the window.

3 Cut another 1½ x 8½-inch (3.8 x 21.6 cm) piece out of the same paper for the back of the bookmark.

4 Using the card stock with the contrasting pattern, cut a 1½ x 8½-inch (3.8 x 21.6 cm) piece for the center of the bookmark.

5 Place the card stock with the cutout window right side down on a work surface. Place the vellum face down on it so that the saying shows through the window. Use two small bits of masking tape to hold the vellum in position.

6 Cut a short length of ribbon, notch one end, and use a small piece of masking tape to attach it to one end of the card stock.

7 Center the top piece (the one that has the vellum taped to it) right side up over the contrasting piece of card stock. Use little pieces of masking tape to hold everything in position.

8 Machine stitch the pieces together with a decorative stitch (the one used for this project was a featherstitch) along the outer line of the top piece of card stock. Carefully remove all the pieces of masking tape that are showing.

9 Trim the outer edges if they're not perfectly aligned.

A BOOK IS A GARDEN, AN ORCHARD, A STOREHOUSE, A PARTY, A COMPANY BY THE WAY, A COUNSELOR, A MULTITUDE OF COUNSELORS.   —HENRY WARD BEECHER

DESIGNER
Nathalie Mornu

Look Smart Portfolio

Show off your good taste while showing off your résumé, work samples, or references. This attractive portfolio is an impressive way to protect and store special documents inside a briefcase, and it makes a great gift for grads.

You Will Need

- Ruler
- Scissors
- Thai paper in a variety of colors
- Pencil
- Sewing machine
- Sewing thread in a variety of colors
- Bone folder
- Craft glue
- Hand-sewing needle
- 2 buttons
- Wax thread

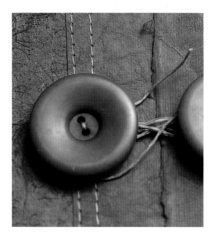

Instructions

1 Cut strips of paper, each 14 inches (35.6 cm) long, in a variety of widths.

2 Overlap the strips in a row to create a sheet that is 14 x 22$\frac{1}{2}$ inches (35.6 x 57.2 cm). Mark the folds at 9-inch (22.9 cm) intervals for the front, back, and short flap. It is a good idea to avoid a seam at the two 9-inch (22.9 cm) marks.

3 Machine stitch the strips together along the 14-inch (35.6 cm) seams.

4 Once everything is sewn together, use a bone folder to score and fold over the two 9-inch (22.9) marks to create the front, back, and flap of the folder.

5 Lay the piece flat again and cut away 1 inch (2.5 cm) on each side along the 22$\frac{1}{2}$-inch (57.2 cm) dimension, leaving the 9 inches (22.9 cm) between the flap and the front to fold over as a gluing tab.

6 Fold the piece down; line up the glue tabs, and glue together.

7 Sew on the decorative buttons for the closure with the wax thread.

8 Once the piece is folded and glued down, you can sew along the 9-inch (22.9 cm) edge to reinforce the sides. Note: Make sure the flap is open before sewing the edge.

Picture Mat Board

This mat board has an interesting texture and looks great as the backdrop for a black and white photograph.

You Will Need

- Black card stock
- White card stock
- Glue stick
- Craft knife (optional)
- Raffia
- Embroidery needle with large eye
- Straight pin
- Double-sided tape (optional)
- Photo of your choice
- Picture frame with narrow black border

Instructions

1 Tear the black card stock into strips, ranging from 1/2-inch (1.3 cm) to 1-inch-long (2.5 cm) pieces. When tearing, put the right side toward you, then flip the card stock over and tear so there will be rough edges facing the same way.

2 On the white card stock, arrange the black strips in a way that pleases you, then glue the strips in place. If you want to drop a picture in the center of the mat board and use it as a frame, cut the paper strips out of the center with the craft knife.

3 Pull the raffia apart into thin pieces about 36 inches (91.4 cm) long so that you don't have to tie knots in the center of the piece.

4 Thread the raffia onto the needle and tie a knot in the end. It's helpful to pierce the paper first with a straight pin before stitching with the embroidery needle. Start at the very end of the piece and stitch up from the back. Place your next stitch about 1/2 inch (1.3 cm) further up and stitch down to the back. Now come back up about 1/4 inch (6 mm) from the last stitch. Once you have the stitch size down, you can use the straight pin to poke the pattern a little ahead of the raffia stitching. It's helpful to have something soft underneath the paper, such as a towel, pillow, or mousepad, to help poke through. Stitch all the way to the other end, tie a knot, and cut the raffia close to the knot.

5 If you have cut the mat out of the middle, just tie a knot at the end, and then start at the other end with a knot. If the knot shows, just place a bit of glue underneath the mat, lay the knot in the glue, and hold it there until it sticks.

6 Repeat the stitching on each black strip.

7 Either glue or use double-sided tape to stick the photo in place.

DESIGNER
Joan K. Morris

Paper Sachets

Filled with lavender or any other dried herb mixture, these sachets are a great addition to your dresser drawer and make a wonderful gift. Simple rice paper and other handmade papers are an elegant choice, but you can add to their appeal with rubber-stamped designs that are uniquely your own.

You Will Need

- Rubber stamp
- Stamping ink
- Unryu papers in white and bright colors
- Markers
- Scissors
- Decorative-edge scissors
- Straight pins
- Sewing machine
- Thread
- Hand-sewing needle (optional)
- Dried herbs or potpourri mix

Instructions

1 Rubber stamp designs onto the white paper, then use markers to add a punch of color to the designs.

2 Cut out simple geometric shapes (squares, rectangles, or triangles) with scissors. A 4-inch (10 cm) shape is a good size to start with.

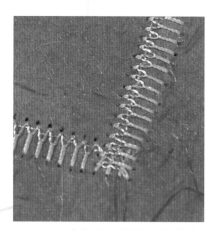

3 Use decorative-edge scissors to cut out a larger shaped piece of colored paper.

4 Pin two pieces together. Machine stitch three sides, and leave one side open. (You can hand-stitch them if you wish).

5 Fill the stitched sachets with a few scoops of dried herbs or potpourri.

6 Sew the last side closed.

Chopstick Holder

A nice touch for any table setting that includes chopsticks, this chopstick holder can be made in colors that complement your place mats and can be used again and again.

You Will Need

- Scrap card stock
- Scissors
- Pencil
- 1 sheet of textured paper, 8½ x 11 inches (21.6 x 27.9 cm)
- 1 sheet of card stock, 8½ x 11 inches (21.6 x 27.9 cm)
- Regular sewing thread
- Embroidery needle
- Sewing machine
- Ice pick
- White craft glue

Instructions

1 Cut an 8½ x 11-inch (21.6 x 27.9 cm) piece of scrap card stock in half so that it measures 8½ x 5½ inches (21.6 x 14 cm). Practice rolling up the shape. Roll from the short end of the paper at the bottom corner. Fold over the top edges to create the opening. When you are happy with the shape, unroll the card stock. This will be your pattern.

2 Using the pattern, cut out the textured paper. Next cut out the solid-color card stock, ¼ inch (6 mm) smaller than the textured paper.

3 Place the textured and solid papers together and roll them up to see how they fit. Open them up and machine stitch all the way around, close to the edge of the solid-color paper. Stitch all the way around again a little closer to the center, in a decorative stitch.

4 Fold the flaps into the proper position and roll up the piece. At the top where the pieces intersect, hand-stitch to hold in place.

5 At the bottom, hand stitch through all the layers to secure the point of the cone.

DESIGNER
Joan K. Morris

Textured Place Mat

Because this place mat is laminated, you can use it indoors or outdoors, and simply wipe it clean when you're done.

You Will Need

Large-scale paper cutter (optional; usually found at full-service copy shops)

Scissors

Paper in color of your choice

Lamination film (available at full-service copy shops)

Tape measure or ruler

Felt-tip pen

Foam, mouse pad, folded fleece, or other cushioning surface

Needle with large eye and very pointed tip

Embroidery threads in color(s) of your choice

Mini hole punch

Instructions

1 Determine the size you want your place mat to be (this one is 13¼ x 19 inches [33.7 x 48.3 cm]). Make it larger or smaller to suit your table, or even round, square, or oval.

2 Use a large paper cutter or scissors to trim the paper to the size and shape you want. This can be done at home or at a local full-service copy shop.

3 Bring the cut paper to a full-service copy shop and have it heat laminated. You may either trim the lamination close to the paper, as shown, or leave a clear plastic border. The latter option keeps the paper more water-resistant over time.

4 Determine where you wish to place the first sewn spiral on the laminated paper. Start with a small size spiral (1 inch [2.5 cm] in diameter) placed in the very center of the laminated paper. Use a tape measure to find and a felt-tip pen to mark the center of the paper. Place the paper on top of the cushioned surface. Use the sharp tip of the needle to puncture the paper at the marked point.

5 Measure and mark points that are ½ inch (1.3 cm) above, below, to the left, and to the right of the first, center hole. Place the paper back on the cushion and use the needle to puncture these points. Using these points as a guide for the size of the spiral, begin puncturing the paper at ⅛-inch (3 mm) intervals, keeping the line round as you work toward the next guide point. Once you have puncture marks for one full circle, move inside the line and make a second, smaller circle. Continue to puncture the paper, spiraling in this manner, until you reach the original, center hole.

(Instructions continue on page 94)

Textured Place Mat

6 Thread the needle with one color of embroidery thread (olive was used here), and tie a knot to secure the end. Beginning under the paper, bring the needle up through one punctured hole on the outside ring of the circle. Pull the thread completely through the hole. Feed the needle down through the second hole away, skipping one hole. Feed the needle up through the skipped hole and then down, skipping one hole. Continue sewing in this pattern until you cover the entire spiral and come to the center of the circle. Tie off the thread under the paper and trim off the excess.

7 Determine where you wish to place the second, larger sewn spiral on the laminated paper. The designer used a spiral that was 2 inches (5.1 cm) in diameter and placed the center of it 4 inches (10.2 cm) from the center of the first, smaller spiral on the same horizontal plane. Use a tape measure to find and a felt-tip pen to mark this point. Place the paper on top of the cushioned surface. Use the sharp tip of the needle to puncture the paper at the marked point.

8 Repeat steps 5 and 6 to puncture and sew the second, larger hole, using the embroidery thread color of your choice. Then, repeat this entire process, adding smaller and larger sewn spirals, until you fill one horizontal row on the place mat.

9 The upper and lower horizontal rows of spirals are punctured and sewn $3^1/2$ inches (8.9 cm) above and below the centerline respectively. For this project, matching spirals (in size and color) were sewn diagonally to their centerline counterparts. The spirals on these lines are also 4 inches (10.2 cm) apart from center point to center point.

10 The place mat is edged with a decorative stitched border. To do this, use a mini hole punch to run two lines of small holes down each edge of the mat. These holes start $3/8$ inch (1 cm) in from each corner and are $3/8$ inch (1 cm) apart, both from the next hole and from the other row.

11 Thread a needle with embroidery thread and tie a knot in the end to secure. Beginning at the first hole on the right side of the bottom row, feed the needle up from under the mat and pull the thread tight. Feed the needle down through the second hole on the top row and pull the thread tight. Continue to stitch on this diagonal until one edge of the mat is complete. (On the reverse side, the edging will be a straight loop stitch.)

12 At the corner, cross the thread to stitch an X shape and proceed with the edging stitch down the next edge. Tie off the thread and start with a new length as needed. Continue stitching until all the edges are complete.

Style-To-Go Take-Out Box

This stylish container, modeled after the familiar Chinese take-out box, can serve a range of functions, from a desktop pencil-holder to kitchen cutlery-holder, to a purpose closer to its origins: an attractive carrier to send home with your guests, filled with special treats.

DESIGNERS

Joan K. Morris
(large box)

Jen Swerington
(smaller boxes)

Style-To-Go Box

- Template on page 122 or Chinese take-out box to use as a pattern
- Patterned paper
- Large piece of white poster board
- Poster board in color that coordinates with the patterned paper
- Matching thread
- Small eyelets
- Scissors
- Sewing machine
- Pencil
- Ruler
- Hole punch

Instructions

For the Large Box

1. If you don't have a box to use as a template, copy the template on page 122, enlarging it to the desired size for your take-out box. Trace around it on the poster board to make a pattern. You'll need to bend some wire for a handle later on. If you have a take-out box, unfold it and take out the wire handle.

2. Lay four pieces of patterned paper out in a square. All four corners should meet in the center. Overlap two of the pieces by about $1/2$ inch (1.3 cm) and machine zigzag stitch them together. Repeat with the other two pieces of paper. Now line up the two pieces you stitched together and overlap them by $1/2$ inch (1.3 cm), and zigzag stitch the whole thing. Tip: As you stitch the paper together, you will need to roll up the paper on the right so it will fit through the sewing machine.

3. Lay the open box or poster board pattern on top of the sewn paper with the stitching in the center and lined up in the center of each flap. Draw around the box and cut out the paper. On the flaps that have the closure, don't cut the line to the center until later. They are difficult to line up.

4. Place the cutout patterned paper on the poster board and cut out a rough square of poster board.

5. Place the poster board back on the wrong sides together. With the paper side up, machine zigzag stitch all the way around the edge.

6. Carefully cut out the poster board so you don't cut any of the stitches.

7. Using the take-out box as a guide, fold your stitched paper in the same way. Start in the center and work your way out. You will see what direction to fold each part.

8 When the folds are complete. Place a small rivet in each side to hold the box together and place the handle.

9 To create the closure, fold the top down and find the center where they intersect and mark with a pencil. Punch a hole in the top one and then mark the bottom one and punch it out. Cut from the edge of the closure straight across to the punched out hole. They will fit together.

10 Insert the handle in the sides and pinch in place.

Light Fantastic Votive Shades

Soft candlelight filters through the perforations in these votive shades, making beautiful shadows that lend ambience to any occasion. If you can't find perforated paper, you can always create your own using decorative hole punches.

DESIGNER
Joan K. Morris

You Will Need

Ruler

Small glass votive
  candleholders

Scissors

2 sheets of vellum,
  8½ x 11 inches
  (21.6 x 27.9 cm)

Large sheet of
  perforated paper

Embroidery needle

Black embroidery floss

Hole punch

Instructions

1 Measure the glass votive holders. Cut out the vellum 1 inch (2.5 cm) larger than the diameter and to the exact height of the votive holders.

2 Cut out the perforated paper, larger than the votive holders by 1 inch (2.5 cm) around and ½ inch (1.3) from top to bottom.

3 Place the vellum on the wrong side of the perforated paper with the extra width at the bottom. Fold the extra perforated paper over the vellum.

4 Hand-stitch a chain stitch with the embroidery needle and the black floss about ½ inch (1.3 cm) up from the bottom.

5 Hand-stitch a blanket stitch at the top edge.

6 Wrap the paper around the glass votive holder and fold over ½ inch (1.3 cm) at each end so the sides meet.

7 Punch five or six holes evenly on each side. Starting at the bottom, lace up the holes with embroidery floss and tie the floss at the top. You can do this while the paper is off the glass holder, and then slide the glass votive under the finished shade.

Stitched Paper Lanterns

Once regarded as disposable party props, paper lanterns have made their way into many homes as permanent light fixtures. If you're planning on having one hang around for a while, why not dress it up with some decorative stitches that completely change its look?

You Will Need

- Store-bought paper lantern with wire support (included in lantern kit)*
- Pencil
- Heavy thread or embroidery floss
- Hand-sewing needle with a large eye
- Nail clippers

Note: *Look for a lantern that has an opening large enough to fit your hand inside.*

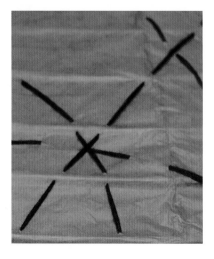

Instructions

1 Open the lantern completely by inserting the wire support. Work with the lantern open at all times.

2 Lightly draw the main lines you plan to stitch on the paper (carefully!).

3 Run two or three strands of floss through the needle, doubling them over by knotting all the ends together. (For this project, three threads were used, then doubled over and knotted at the end, creating a 6-ply thread.) Make a fat knot at the end that will not pull through the delicate paper.

4 Begin stitching at the narrow opening of the lantern where two pieces of paper have been overlapped for further strength. Start by pulling the thread through from the inside, so the knot is inside the lantern. When stitching, pull the thread gently because the paper is delicate and can tear easily.

5 For faster stitching, pass the needle under the wire ribs and back up while gently compressing the lantern.

6 To tie off the threads inside the lantern, pass the needle under a nearby wire rib and create a loop, then pass the thread through the loop and gently pull to make a knot. Clip the thread with nail clippers (this is much easier than trying to get scissors inside).

7 Continue stitching until the design flows all around the lantern.

(Instructions continue on page 102)

Stitched Paper Lanterns

To Make the Circles:

1 Lightly trace around the lid to make as many circles as you want on the decorative paper (you'll probably need about 20 circles). Cut out the circles.

2 Fold each circle in half and cut a small shape out of the center. Use the awl or needle to pierce six holes around each circle.

3 Open the lantern completely with the wire support. Work with the lantern open at all times.

4 Draw the main lines you plan to stitch very lightly on the lantern, and draw a small X in each position where you want to place a circle (it's a good idea to put the circles in places where

there is overlapping paper for extra strength).

5 Run two or three strands of floss through the needle, doubling them over by knotting all the ends together. (For this project, three threads were used, then doubled over and knotted at the end, creating a 6-ply thread.) Make a fat knot at the end that will not pull through the delicate paper.

6 Begin stitching at the narrow opening of the lantern where two pieces of paper have been overlapped for further strength. Start by pulling the thread through from the inside, so the knot is inside the lantern. When stitching, pull the thread gently, because the paper is delicate and can tear easily.

7 For faster stitching, pass the needle under the wire ribs and back up while gently compressing the lantern.

8 When you reach an X, pull the thread through one hole in the circle and stitch the circle to the lantern, forming a star with three stitches in the middle of the circle. The trick here is to keep any back-connecting stitches behind the opaque decorative paper because they can be seen through the translucent paper lantern.

9 Continue stitching along the lines you drew to the next X. Sew on the circle and continue to the end, stitching a decorative motif, then tie off threads inside. Note: To tie off the threads inside the lantern, pass the needle under a nearby wire rib and create a loop, then pass the thread through the loop and gently pull to make a knot. Clip the thread with nail clippers (this is much easier than trying to get scissors inside).

10 Continue stitching until the design flows all around the lantern.

Shade Upgrade

Here's an inexpensive way to get custom window shades: Buy an inexpensive paper shade and reimagine it with stitching and paper embellishments that complement your décor. Don't be afraid to really go for it with the stitching—it won't tear if you're careful!

You Will Need

- Purchased paper window shade
- Masking tape or packing tape
- Decorative paper of your choice
- Straight pins
- Sewing machine
- Contrasting thread
- Scissors

Instructions

1 Open up the paper shade and lay it out completely flat. Move the drawstrings up to the top and out of the way. Tape them securely so they won't get stitched down.

2 Place the decorative paper on the shade, moving it around until you hit on the design you like. Pin it down with straight pins when you're happy with the design.

3 Roll up one end of the shade. Start sewing at one end of the top of the shade, back-tack your first few stitches, then stitch horizontal lines across the shade. Back-tack at the end of each stitched line as well. Play with decorative stitches, and as you pass over the decorative paper, stitch along the sides to secure it to the shade. Remove the pins as you go.

4 Add more stitching to embellish the center of the decorative paper or throughout open areas.

5 As you progress from the top to the bottom of the shade, roll the finished area so that you can work in the middle. Essentially, the shade becomes a big scroll that is flat in the middle area so that it will fit in the sewing machine.

6 Embellish the top overhanging flap with more stitches in the same manner as the main part of the shade.

7 Trim all the thread tails. Remove the tape from the drawstrings and place them back around the shade, making sure that the shade functions properly.

Starry Night-Light Shade

Who could be afraid of the dark with such a dreamy night-light to light the way?
Plain night-light shades can be found in craft stores, just waiting for you to
transform them with starry paper, beads, and silvery thread.

You Will Need

Purchased night light

Scrap paper

Pencil

Scissors

Sheet of star-pattern
   vellum,
   8½ x 11 inches
   (21.6 x 27.9 cm)

Embroidery needle

Silver metallic
   embroidery thread

Clear glass beads

Instructions

1 Lay the night-light shade on a piece of scrap paper and draw around the edge to create a pattern (you'll need to roll the shade as you draw). Cut out the pattern, check to see that it fits the shade, and adjust as necessary.

2 Once you have a pattern that fits, cut the patterned vellum, using the scrap paper template as a guide.

3 With the needle and thread, stitch the glass beads onto the vellum, positioning the beads in between the stars.

4 Blanket stitch the vellum pattern to the shade all the way around the edge. Hide the knots in back of the shade. Stitch from front to back, with the stitches almost on top of each other, to create a strong binding. Now start a blanket stitch and go all the way around the edge until you get to the opening. Stitch around at this point and knot the end, hiding the knot.

Adorable Door Sign

A kid's room is his or her castle—the only room in the house where he or she's in charge. A fun door sign is like a gatekeeper to control traffic in and out of the inner chamber. This neat design allows you to choose from several different messages attached to the back piece, which spins around so that the message shows through the window in the front piece.

You Will Need

- Compass
- 2 sheets of paper, about 12 inches (30.5 cm) square
- Ruler
- Pencil
- Scissors
- Thread
- Sewing machine
- Coordinating thread
- Craft knife
- Hole punch
- Computer with printer
- 5 or 6 sheets of various print papers
- White scrap paper
- Brad
- Masking tape
- Ribbon

Instructions

1 For the front part of the sign, draw a circle on a sheet of paper, then extend two lines from opposite sides so that you have a rectangular shape on one side and a circle on the other. Cut it out then machine stitch along the edges in a decorative stitch. Lightly pencil in the child's name, the word "is," a colon, and the shape of the

window. Cut out the window, and stitch along its edges. Stitch the words. Punch two holes in each corner.

2 For the back part of the sign, draw a circle with a diameter 1/2 inch (1.3 cm) wider than the original circle on the second sheet of paper. Cut it out. Machine stitch along its edges with a decorative stitch.

3 Print the words for five or six different activities— sleeping, at school, playing, watching TV, etc.—on the pieces of paper with various patterns. Use a variety of fonts and sizes, experimenting first on white scrap paper to make sure they'll fit inside the window you cut out in the front piece of the sign.

4 After you print the final versions of the words, cut them out in dimensions slightly smaller than the window in the front piece of the sign.

5 Cut a tiny "X" in the centers of both circles. To assemble the sign, align the Xs and slip the brad through them, working from front to back, then open the brad. Use a couple of small pieces of tape to attach one of the words to the circle so it appears in the window. Turn the circle a bit so that the word is no longer showing, and attach a second word so it appears in the window. Repeat with all the words that will fit.

6 Disassemble the front from the back of the sign. Stitch down all the words. Reassemble the sign. Slip the ribbon through the punched holes in the corners of the sign and secure with a knot or bow.

DESIGNER
Nathalie Mornu

Beaded Lampshade

Certain paper designs just call out for three-dimensional embellishments. The charming lantern design on this paper, for example, was enhanced by a chain stitch to join the lanterns together, as well as beads to make them a bit more playful. Look for paper that inspires you, and use your imagination.

You Will Need

Ruler

Scissors

Sheet of plastic for a thin template, 12 x 18 inches (30.5 x 45.7 cm)

Large sheet of decorative paper

Large paper clips

Lamp base

Pencil

Hole punch

Lightbulb clip

Embroidery needle

Black embroidery floss

Assorted small black beads

Black thread

Glue stick

2 lengths of stiff, bendable wire

Wire cutters

Instructions

1 Cut the plastic sheet in half, so that it measures 9 x 12 inches (22.9 x 30.5 cm).

2 Cut the decorative paper into two pieces, each 10 1/2 x 14 inches (26.7 x 35.6 cm), making sure the pattern is oriented in the correct direction for your lamp.

3 Place one of the decorative papers on one of the plastic templates. Fold the top of the paper over 1/2 inch (1.3 cm), fold the bottom over 1 inch (2.5 cm), and fold the sides over 1 inch (2.5 cm). Mark a dot every 1/2 inch (1.3 cm) along each edge.

4 Punch holes on the dots through the paper and the template. Repeat steps 1 through 4 with the other piece of decorative paper and the other plastic template.

5 Remove the patterned paper from the templates. Measure down 2 inches (5.1 cm) from the center top of each template. This is where you will attach the sides of the bulb clip. With the side of the bulb clip in place, mark four spots that you'll punch through for the arms of the bulb clip.

6 Stitch around the arm of the bulb clip and the template with embroidery floss until the template is securely attached. Repeat for the other side of the bulb clip and the other template.

7 Chain stitch between patterns on the paper with embroidery thread.

(Instructions continue on page 112)

Beaded Lampshade

8 Stitch on the beads with the regular black thread. You will need to tie each one separately because the thread will show through the lamp when the light is on. Cut the thread close to the knot.

9 Glue the decorative papers to the template pieces. Wrap the top and sides over and glue in place. Leave the bottom open.

10 Place the two sides of the shade together, matching up the holes. Stitch down each side with black embroidery floss. At the top, leave 8 inches (20.3 cm) of thread at the end of the knot. Wrap the thread around each piece twice to secure. At the bottom, tie a knot and leave 8 inches (20.3 cm) of floss. Take the floss from the top and tie a knot with the floss from the bottom on the inside of the lampshade and push it to the edge to hide it. Stitch the other side the same way.

11 Bend the wire to the shape of the top of the lamp. Cut it to the correct length with wire cutters. Place it in the bottom of the shade and fold and glue the paper over the wire to hold in place.

12 To hide where the bulb clip was stitched, cut two ovals from your decorative paper, each a little bigger than the size of the stitching. Cut a slit in each oval to slide over the wire of the bulb clip. Glue the ovals in place.

Flower Girl Handbag

Imagine this delicate handbag filled with flowers and carried by a bridesmaid or even used as a table centerpiece at a wedding reception. Although it may be too fragile to withstand day-to-day use, this purse is great for special occasions or decorative use.

Flower Girl Handbag

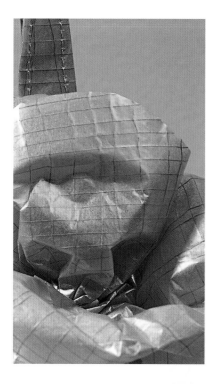

You Will Need

Ruler

Scissors

Large sheet of coated, textured paper

Pencil

Sewing machine

Matching thread

2 pieces of floral paper for lining

Straight pins

1 yard (91.4 cm) of ribbon, 1/2 inch (1.3 cm) wide

Embroidery needle

Instructions

1 Measure and cut two 8 1/2 x 11-inch (21.6 x 27.9 cm) pieces from the coated paper and place them right sides together. Measure and cut two 2-inch (5.1 cm) squares from the bottom corners of the paper.

2 Open up the cut pieces, and place the pieces wrong side up, with the cut bottom edges overlapping 1/2 inch (1.3 cm). Machine stitch these together. Fold the two pieces up about 2 inches (5 cm) in from the stitching. This starts forming the purse. Machine stitch the two side seams together, about 1/8 inch (3 mm) in from the edge. The stitching will be on the right side. Fold the stitched seam to the front on both sides.

3 Fold the 2-inch (5.1 cm) squares in to create the bottom of the purse. Machine stitch these seams 1/8 inch (3 mm) from the edge. This is the basic bag.

4 Repeat steps 1, 2, and 3 on the lining paper, except reverse the paper so the right sides are facing in.

5 Carefully slide the lining into the purse.

6 To make the handles, cut two 3 x 13-inch (7.6 x 33 cm) pieces from the coated paper. Fold these pieces in half lengthwise, fold the edges in to the center, and fold again at the first fold. Machine stitch both edges the whole length.

7 Decide where you want to place the handles. Position them between the coated paper and the lining, and pin them in place.

8 Machine stitch all the way around the top edge of the purse, close to the edge.

9 Cut two pieces of ribbon the length around the top edge of the purse.

10 Pin the ribbon in place, one ribbon around the outside edge and one around the inside. Hand-stitch in place.

11 To make the flower, cut two 3 x 11-inch (7.6 x 27.9 cm) pieces from the coated paper. Cut scallops along one of the long edges of both pieces. There should be about five scallops per edge.

12 Place the scalloped pieces together and machine baste the other edge of the pieces. Gather the basting and roll the edges around to create the flower. Hand-stitch the bottom of the flower to keep the shape.

13 Hand-stitch the flower onto the purse.

Paper Menagerie Mobile

A sweet gift idea, this mobile takes advantage of the many patterned papers available in pastel prints. Parents will appreciate it as a charming and safe choice for a nursery mobile–there are no small parts to fall off and cause a choking hazard.

You Will Need

White card stock, 8¹/₂ x 11 inches (21.6 x 27.9 cm)

Pencil

Scissors

Templates on page 124

Assorted pastel-print papers, 8¹/₂ x 11 inches (21.6 x 27.9 cm)

Scrap paper

Glue stick

Matching thread

Sewing machine

Embroidery needle

Embroidery floss, 1 skein each of black and white

Hole punch

Plastic-coated hanger

Patterned scrapbook paper, 12 x 12 inches (30.5 x 30.5 cm)

Narrow white ribbon, 36 inches (91.4 cm) long

¹/₂-inch-wide (1.3 cm) satin ribbon, 24 inches (61 cm) long

Instructions

1 On the scrap card stock, draw and cut out the templates on page 124. Cut out separate pieces for the manes, ears, and tails.

2 Choose the print papers you want to use for each animal. Cut out two of each piece by folding the paper in half and cutting both pieces at the same time.

3 Glue the card stock cutouts to the wrong side of one of the paper animals, and glue it to the other side. Glue on the manes, tails, and ears.

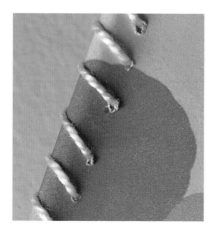

4 Machine stitch with a straight stitch around each animal, close to the edge, then stitch around the ears, manes, and tails.

5 With the black embroidery floss, make a French knot (see page 15) as an eye for each animal.

6 Punch a hole in the top of each animal, positioning the hole so that the animal hangs straight down.

7 Lay the hanger on the wrong side of the patterned scrapbook paper. Draw around the hanger, leaving a ¹/₂-inch (1.3 cm) margin. Place the paper right sides together and cut out the hanger shape.

8 Run the glue around the wrong-side edge of the cut paper. Lay the hanger on the paper, and wrap it around the edges. Repeat with the paper for the other side.

9 With the white embroidery floss, stitch around the entire edge of the paper-covered hanger.

10 Punch three holes evenly across the bottom of the hanger.

11 Cut three pieces of satin ribbon to the length you want the animals to hang. Tie the ribbon to the holes in the animals, then to the holes in the hanger.

12 Tie a piece of the satin ribbon in a bow around the top of the hanger.

DESIGNER
Joan K. Morris

Switch-Plate Covers

A fun way to add a little color and pattern to your wall, these switch-plate covers are easy to make. The free-form designs allow you to be spontaneous and be inspired by the paper you choose.

You Will Need

- Ruler
- Switch-plate cover
- Sharpened or mechanical pencil
- Decorative or found paper (old magazine or book pages, dress patterns, etc)
- Scissors
- Bone folder
- Sewing machine
- Contrasting thread
- Craft knife with sharp blades and cutting mat
- Glue stick
- Small paintbrush or craft brush
- Small container clear acrylic gloss medium

Instructions

1 Measure the outside dimensions of the switch-plate cover. Add $1^{1}/_{2}$ inches (3.8 cm) to the dimensions, which allows for a $^{3}/_{4}$-inch (1.9 cm) border on each side. Mark this measurement on decorative paper and cut it out.

2 Center the switch plate (face down) on the decorative paper rectangle. Lightly trace the switch and screw holes with pencil.

3 Fold sides of paper up around switch plate and score them with the bone folder. Now you can see where the pattern of the decorative paper needs to be positioned on the switch-plate cover.

4 Machine stitch the paper in the design of your choice. Experiment with various decorative stitches, free-motion embroidery, or variegated threads, following or contrasting the paper's pattern. To minimize thread tails and possible unraveling, always start sewing from the edge of the paper, and be mindful of the areas that will be cut out (switch holes) or folded back.

Trim the thread tails when you're done.

5 Using the craft knife, carefully cut out the switch holes. Don't poke through the screw holes yet.

(Instructions continue on page 120)

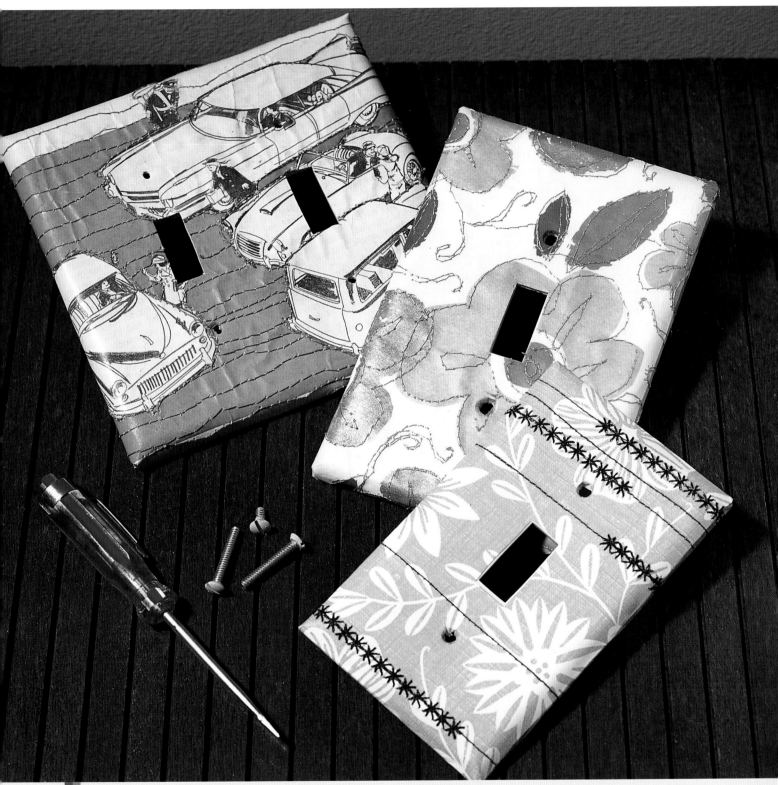

Switch Plate Covers

6 Apply glue to the entire front of the switch plate. Lay the paper on top, lining up the holes. Burnish the paper with the bone folder and flatten it across the front.

7 Trim off the corners with a clean, diagonal slice, but (very important!) leave about a 1/4-inch (6 mm) overhang so that the corner is not exposed.

8 Apply glue to the two side panels of the paper. Wrap the paper tightly around the back of the plate. Burnish it with the bone folder.

9 At the ends of the side panels that have been folded in, use the tip of the bone folder to knock in or push the paper around the corners. This makes a clean, well-sealed corner.

10 Apply glue to the top and bottom panels of paper. Wrap them tightly around to the back of the plate. Burnish them with the bone folder.

11 Using the pencil, poke through the screw holes.

12 To protect the paper from dirty hands, brush on a coat or two of clear acrylic gloss medium and let it dry.

Templates

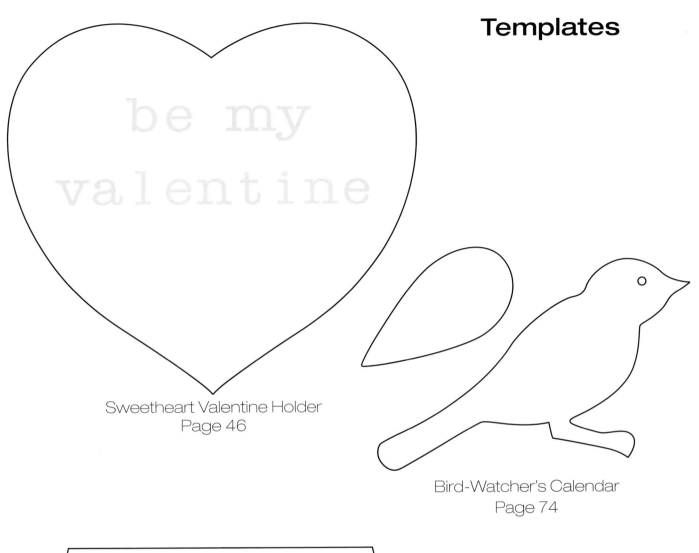

be my
valentine

Sweetheart Valentine Holder
Page 46

Bird-Watcher's Calendar
Page 74

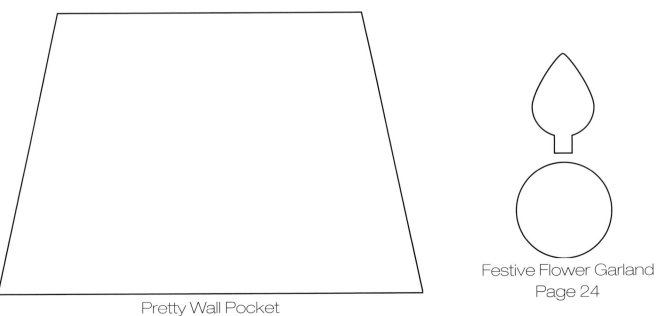

Pretty Wall Pocket
Page 79

Festive Flower Garland
Page 24

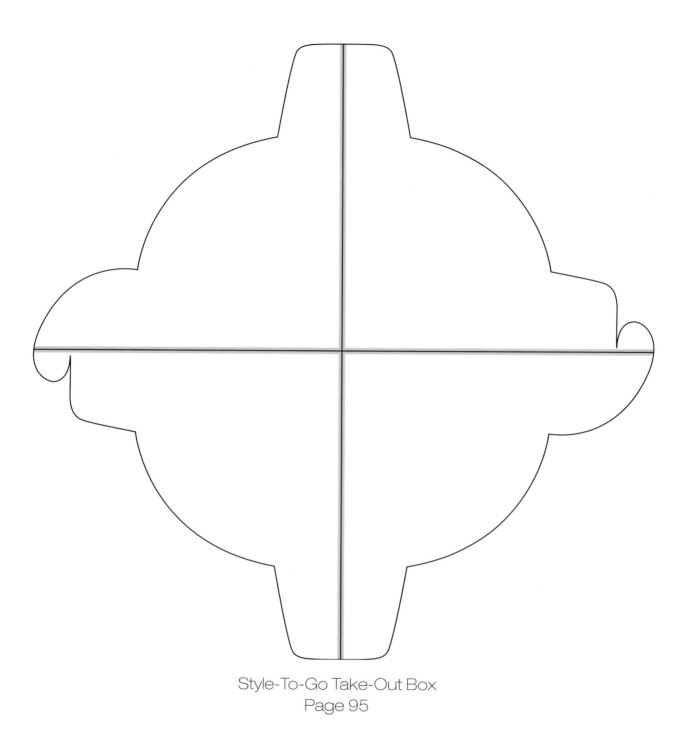

Style-To-Go Take-Out Box
Page 95

Stitched Stockings
Page 36

Paper Menagerie Mobile
Page 117

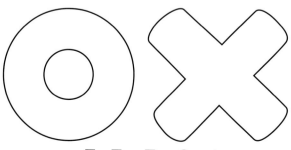

Tic-Tac-Toe Card
Page 62

Fashion Friends
Page 32

Modern-Life Lampshade
Page 34

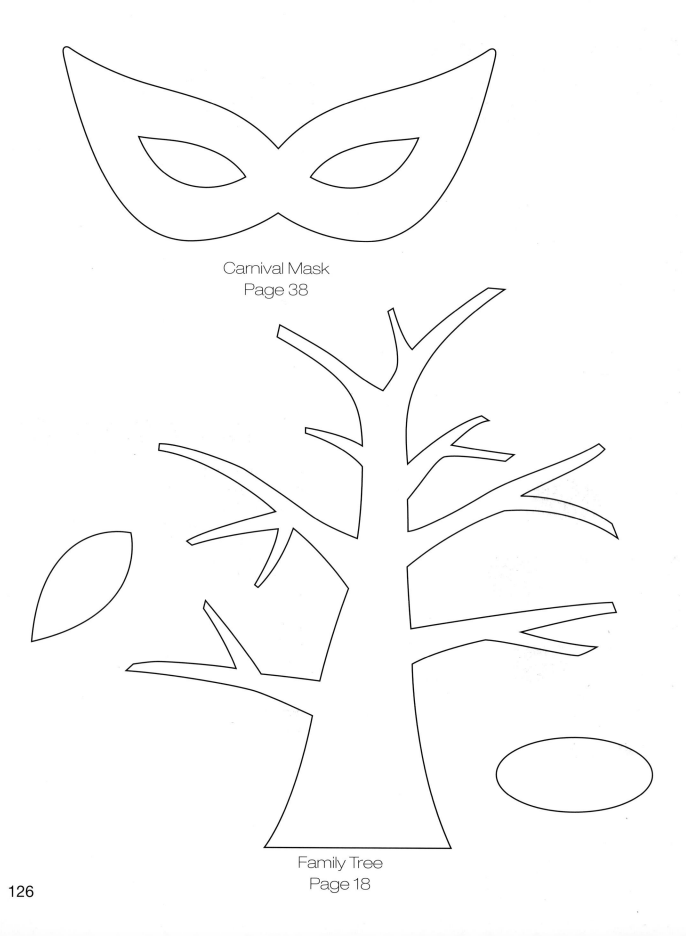

Carnival Mask
Page 38

Family Tree
Page 18